ALSO BY PAM

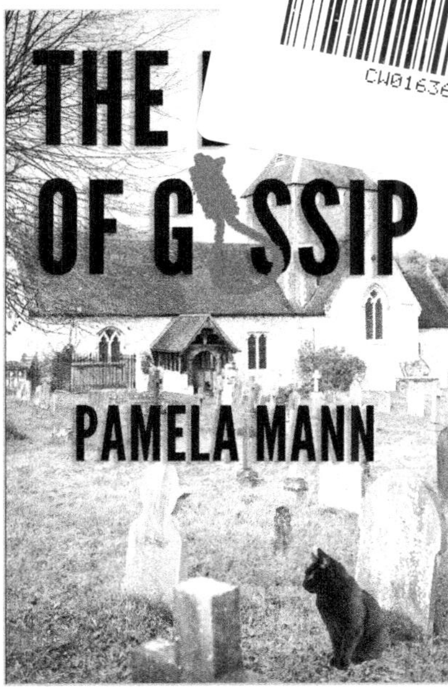

Religious unrest reigns in 16th century England.

Expert midwife, Margory, has lost no babies or mothers in childbirth so gossip accuses her of witchcraft.

Even she isn't sure whether she has special powers.

All Margory wants is a man to love who loves her and children of her own.

And that's what she intends to have, whatever the cost.

A TRUE to LIFE PERIOD NOVEL of a
YOUNG WOMAN'S TRIUMPH OVER ADVERSITY

To Anne
with love
Pamela
x

PAMELA MANN

MEN RULE

This edition first published in paperback by
Michael Terence Publishing in 2023
www.mtp.agency

ISBN 9781800945616

Michael Terence
Publishing

Chapter 1

Hertfordshire, England
Winter 1564

Fog was creeping damply into every corner of the vast manor house, seeping into Margory's bones. She shivered, despite the huge fire, and rang the bell. Something was not quite right about Lucy's visit.

"Yes, Mistress." Goodwife Sykes hobbled into the library slowly, dragging her feet a little, prompting Margory to think, not for the first time, that her loyal housekeeper was beginning to look much older now. When one saw a person every day, these sorts of things could easily go unnoticed. She would start to give her fewer duties.

"Please ask one of the servants to take Lucy to a bedchamber in the servants' quarters. Take your bag with you, Lucy. You have got a bag, haven't you? How did you get all this way on your own? You are fortunate to have reached us unscathed. I would suggest that you don't risk such a journey again, alone. I never have known where you are living with Master Arthur and I don't wish to know, but I think it is some distance away, and you look very tired." Margory no longer felt jealousy. Arthur had taken her heart and turned it upside down, emptying it of all feeling for him.

"I left four days ago, Mistress, and packed as much as I could carry on the horse. Master Arthur wouldn't let me have a horse of my own so I had to ask one of the stable lads to saddle up for me and not to tell the Master I'd gone. I didn't like to ask that of him, but I know him to be a kind boy who had sometimes seen my bruises. Master Arthur had stayed out late as usual, drinking, I assume, and doesn't get up until mid-morning."

"What about your children, Lucy? You've got two, haven't you?" Arthur's fateful visit and its even worse news suddenly loomed large in her memory, in spite of the four year interval.

"Oh, they're safe as can be, Mistress Margory. I wouldn't have left otherwise. Little darlings they are, too. I took both to a good friend of mine before I left. She'll take care of them for the moment."

Margory mused again about the explanation for Lucy's flight and why the reason would be so strong that she would leave her small children behind. Surely the bruises she mentioned hadn't been inflicted by Arthur? Clearly, she would like to stay here at The Manor, and that raised even more questions. But this wasn't the time to start asking Lucy: she wasn't the only one who felt very weary.

"Very well, and please close the door as you go out. Wash and rest now, Lucy. Let me see. It's 5 of the clock. Goodwife Sykes, would you ask cook to delay the meal this evening. That will give Lucy time to recover from her long ride before joining the servants for the evening meal. We'll speak again tomorrow morning, Lucy. Oh, and I assume you are happy to join the servants for their meals as you know most, if not all of them?" Margory thought it may be helpful, one of these days, to ask Lucy the circumstances in which she had found herself when living with Arthur. But that could wait.

"Thank you, Mistress. I am suddenly very tired indeed."

Margory lingered for a moment, watching the pair walk slowly across the huge hall. Lucy still had a limp, she noticed. It was all so puzzling. Then, having slid the bolt on the library door - a habit she found difficult to discard – she turned, crossing to the book shelves. Removing one of the books, she pressed the button and watched the familiar sight of the small door sliding back.

Chapter 2

The following morning, Margory sat down alone, a little later than usual, to break her fast at the end of the long dining table. She had hardly slept and couldn't stomach a large meal. The servants had been asked to only serve a small manchet, a piece of salt fish and a few sprats, with an accompanying small ale. Since the ransacking of The Manor, she had begun to save a few bottles of wine again which she used, now, only for special occasions – and there were precious few of those.

Suddenly she remembered, through the haze of her weariness, that Hugh had sent a message saying he would be coming to The Manor later this morning; she knew not the nature of his visit but her spirits immediately lifted. She had known him now for, what was it, a little over three years and, in that time, he had begun to return The Manor to its former splendour. He had also started to transform Margory into someone she liked a little. She wondered again whether her warm feeling was love. But she mustn't allow this indulgence: she put it aside.

"Is that a horse I hear, Goodwife Sykes?"

Margory's rise of hopeful anticipation was quickly dashed, however. No, it couldn't be.

"Master Arthur! Wait a moment, please, while I let mistress know that you're here."

"I'll tell her myself. Out of my way you old woman." Arthur waved his hand dismissively, barely missing the servant who, in stepping back, almost fell.

That familiar, bullying voice. Margory would know it anywhere. First, Lucy, now Arthur. What did he want, she wondered? Perhaps he had come to take Lucy back to their home – wherever that was.

Arthur strode into the library as though his four years of absence didn't exist.

"Well, wife. I see you are still living in style in The Manor. Perhaps not in the style you were used to when growing up. But in a grand house nevertheless."

Giving her no chance to reply, the sound of yet another horse was heard, followed by loud knocking at the great door. Margory heard her faithful servant's delighted greeting.

"Master Hugh. How good to see you." Margory strained to hear as Goodwife Sykes lowered her voice.

"Yes, we have another visitor, sir. Let me show you through into the library."

"No need, Goodwife Sykes. I know where it is, of course, so don't let me detain you from your duties."

"Thank you, sir."

Chapter 3

The soft knock on the library door was, Margory thought, so like Hugh – polite, considerate. Opening it, she tried to give a warning look to the man she now cared for very much.

"Hello, Hugh. How nice to see you. You look rather alarmed. Is everything all right?"

"I came as fast as I could, Margory, to tell you that the Thames has flooded greatly, marshes are overflowing and cattle have been drowned. Not surprisingly, it has inflicted dense fog in this area. I suggest you…"

"And who, may I ask, are you to suggest anything to my wife, whatever the reason? It certainly isn't appropriate, wife, for a married woman to be receiving a man, particularly when that man is on his own."

Hugh's look of surprise displayed his lack of experience in being spoken to in that manner. Margory drew in her breath.

"This is Hugh Taylor. Hugh, this is Arthur Wright."

"Oh and don't let's forget, dear wife, to add that I am your husband. What brings you to my door, or, should I say, to the door of my wife, as you clearly did not know of my presence?"

"That is for Margory to know as you and I have not had the pleasure of being acquainted. May I speak to you alone, Margory?"

"Indeed you may not speak to my wife on your own. Whatever you have to say, you can say here and now. On the other hand, if you cannot, then be on your way."

Margory's knuckles turned white as she clenched her fists. First, the surprise of Lucy's arrival and now the unwelcome appearance of Arthur, after several years. What could he want? Probably money. But if it was, she couldn't help. It was always money that Arthur wanted in order to continue his climb up the social ladder. She was frustrated at not being able to greet Hugh with the warmth she felt and he deserved. Never before had she seen such a look of dislike cross Hugh's face. Her heart plummeted for him.

"Margory. If you would feel more comfortable, I shall leave. I am perfectly happy to do so, but only if you wish it. We can arrange to meet on another occasion. I have news of your friend, the Countess of Shrewsbury's family." Hugh lowered his voice,

"It appears that her brother-in-law, Edward, may be poisoning those who get in his way again."

Straining, but not quite managing to hear, Arthur's face twisted in anger. He spat,

"I think you will not arrange another meeting! My wife will meet only those I give her permission to meet. As your arrival at the home of a married woman is highly questionable, I order you to leave now. And any news of my wife's friends is news I would also wish to hear."

"I'll show you out, Hugh."

"You will stay exactly where you are, wife, and you will only move when I say you can. Do I make myself clear? As for you, Master Taylor or whatever your name is, you clearly know your way out. I can see that you have questions to answer, wife."

Gently touching Margory's hand, Hugh smiled at her,

"Let me know, my dear, when and where you would like to meet and I shall be there. In particular, if you need my help, do please let me know." Hugh's voice was anxious, but all Margory could do was to smile and reciprocate the touch of his hand.

Again, Arthur's face screwed into a knot so tight that Margory wondered how it would regain normality. How clear were the differences between these two men, she thought. One who had used her as a toy, to be discarded and picked up again at his whim, the other, warm, gentle, kind and considerate. Her judgement had certainly been poor all those years ago. And, of course, she knew she wasn't blameless. Unhappily, she watched Hugh leave.

Chapter 4

"So, wife, 'tis fortunate I returned when I did as you seem to have forgotten your marital status. But I'll forgive you – this time. For I'm back and shall take my rightful place at The Manor, both outside the bedchamber and in it.

Margory's eyes widened in horror.

"What do you mean, Arthur, by 'my rightful place'?

"What I mean, dearest, is that, not only will you and I be eating our meals together, but the mother of my children, Lucy, will be joining us at the head of the table, too. One of the grooms told me she had been seen leaving and I assume she is here as she has nowhere else to go. I shall be speaking to her privately about her conduct. But mainly, my love, you and I will be resting in the bed we shared as man and wife. And lest that should still be unclear. We shall be sleeping together. I assume that side of the bed has not been warmed by anyone else in my absence? I shall take your silence as a 'no'. You're looking very tired, Margory. I think that now is a very good time to start our life together once more. Now! This very minute. I trust you have re-stocked the wine cellar and included my favourite claret. Don't let me detain you. I shall join you anon."

Margory sighed. How was she to deal with this new situation? She would need to pray for guidance.

Chapter 5

Margory dragged her feet up the long, winding staircase, wishing it led to Heaven. In fact, she seemed to be approaching Hell. Never had she been so reluctant to take to her bed. Even in the early days of her marriage to Arthur, when she had gradually grown accustomed to his visiting the inn and other, unknown locations, before joining her in bed, she had always longed for their coming together so that children would result. But those days were long gone. At the passing of her parents, she had seen his true colours. At her time of needing him the most, he had left her without money and with unmanaged land – her parents' and grandparents' land. What he had given her was the knowledge that he had loved another and given her a child. Hannah. In that miasmic abyss, at least he had shown that he was capable of loving another human being. But had he loved her more than he loved himself? From what Lucy had said, Arthur had only taken her as mistress and mother as she resembled Hannah, her deceased maid. Poor Lucy. Poor anyone who became entangled in Arthur's web of deceit.

Margory's thoughts were disturbed by a light knocking on the bedchamber door. She had almost reverted to totally preparing herself for sleep as she had had to do when The Manor was reduced to penury following her parents' demise and Arthur's departure.

"Come."

"Oh mistress Margory, are you ill? You look very pale. I'm so sorry that I didn't hear you come to your bed or I would have been here, ready to help you."

"Don't worry, Ruth, I am well but not feeling quite myself at the moment."

The gentle moment crashed.

"Get out of here. I shall deal with my wife's disrobing myself."

Ruth stepped away from Margory quickly.

"Er. You will dis…?"

"That's what I said, and if you don't leave immediately, you will be leaving our employment altogether, without a letter of recommendation. And, as you know, that means no-one would ever employ you again. So get out before I throw you out!"

Margory saw tears welling in Ruth's eyes and, moving quickly to her side, she took her elbow and, steering her to the door of the bedchamber, whispered:

"Don't worry, my dear, all will be well. Go to your bed and thank you for coming to help me. I'll speak to you tomorrow. You're a good maid and very helpful. You won't be leaving here, I promise."

Arthur's shout sent the maid scurrying quickly, like a mouse whose location has been discovered.

"What were you telling her? Not countermanding my order were you? How short is your memory, Margory. I told you before that I won't be commanded by a woman, and certainly not my wife. I do take the part of servants occasionally – having been one myself several years past – but won't have my order reversed by you. You may be high-born, which I was not, but my circumstances changed – and you were partly that instrument of change. I began on the bottom rung of society's ladder and you helped me climb – indeed, you lavished me with opportunities to ascend. I would have done it without you, of course, but you facilitated and hastened my progress, with promises of fleshly delights on the way. But I shall never forget nor, indeed, regret my lowly beginnings. Neither shall I be ruled by servants, particularly those you appear to have befriended. That is totally inappropriate for the wife of the Lord of the Manor."

Chapter 6

1556
Autumn

"Mother, there are holes in my galoshes and these coarse, woollen socks are itchy."

"Well, you've only got one pair of galoshes, Arthur, so they'll have to do. The wooden sole's in one piece, though, isn't it? That's the main thing. Nothing I can do about the socks, unfortunately."

I groaned. It was so unfair. There was a gap the width of several fields between the poor and the rich. Our two-roomed cottage was barely big enough to house mother, father, my little sister and I. Each time I looked out of the window, all I could see was the manor house. The Manor. With its many glazed windows, huge, oak front door and tall chimneys that reached to the sky; rooms that were warm in the winter, and all surrounded by acres and acres of land. Land that my father had worked since he was a boy. And now it seemed that was to be my lot in life, too.

"Arthur and Mary, come here, now, I've something to tell you. Come and sit by me." Mother broke through my reverie. What did she want to tell me that was so important? A few moments later, I couldn't believe my ears. Another baby. In this hovel. Well, I wasn't going to put up with a life like this for much longer. But mother was still speaking.

"Arthur, did you hear what I said? The Lord and Lady of The Manor have said they would like you to help serve the champagne and sweetmeats for Mistress Margory's Confirmation. The butler and cook are going to give you lessons in what you'll need to do. You'll also be given one of the servant's outfits, but just to borrow for the day. Won't you look smart! Would you like that? You remember Mistress Margory, don't you? She came with Lady Francis to deliver Mary two years ago. She wants to deliver babies, too, once she's experienced, then licensed."

"No, I wouldn't like to serve the gentry! Why would I like that? They're nothing but people who think they're better than everybody else."

"Now, Arthur. It's time you realised that they *are* better than us. There are different social classes in England; we're working class and they're the gentry. Think about it, Arthur. You'll get to see the beautiful rooms at The Manor. You'll see the magnificent fireplaces, the pretty pictures and, if you're lucky, you may be able to sample some of the delicious food, too. Wouldn't you like that? You'll also be able to see how the gentry behave."

"I know how they behave, and I don't like it! They walk around with their noses in the air. And why would I want to see inside The Manor?"

"Well, maybe you'd like to work there some time, when you're older. Next year, when you're 16, you could start an apprenticeship to the Lord, perhaps. I've always thought you were a clever boy and that you won't be working on the land with your father forever. Also, some of the maids are pretty. You might like to start walking out with one of them some time."

"Shan't. Ugh! Girls. They're good for nothing."

"Well, don't forget that I was a girl not too long ago, and your father enjoyed walking with me on his arm."

"Yes, but that's different. You're my mother!"

I could have added that, these days, father went straight from the fields to the inn, so we didn't see him much anyway. But for once, I stayed silent.

"Well, think about it, Arthur, because I think you'd like to take the opportunity of seeing inside The Manor. His Lordship is a very nice gentleman, too."

That night, lying on my straw bed, I did think about it. I thought that perhaps I could try it and if I didn't like it I wouldn't have to do it again. Also, I thought, it would be something I could boast about to the friends I worked with in the fields.

Chapter 7

"You're not to talk to any of the people you're serving. D'you understand? They won't be interested in anything you have to say."

"Yes."

"Yes, sir."

"Yes, sir."

"I'm the butler here and if you want to say anything, you say it to me. All right?"

"Yes, sir. But what if…"

"No 'what ifs'. These people are your superiors. They've got lots of money and you've got none. They're gentry and you're a nobody. Is that clear?"

I wriggled. I hadn't realised I was a nobody. I didn't think I liked being a nobody.

"If I'm nobody, how can I put on special clothes and serve the gentry – er – sir?"

"No back chat, lad, or I'll find somebody else to do this. There are lots who want to, so if you can't control your tongue, there are others who can, and what will your mother say then?"

He was right. I knew she'd be disappointed, and I didn't like to see her disappointed. She was a good woman, my mother, with a sensible head on her shoulders. What was the word I was searching for? Respect. I respected her. I could always count on her advice being good. I'd better try to do what this man, the butler, said. But I didn't like it. I wanted to do what I wanted to do, when I wanted to do it. Not follow somebody else's orders. Particularly when they worked in this very big house. What right did the size of a house give somebody to tell me what to do? But I did want to see the rooms here – as well as all the food! My mouth began to water at the thought.

"All right, sir."

"Not 'all right, sir', as though I'm doing you a favour. 'Yes, sir'. I can see I shall have to watch you – as though I haven't enough to do. And if I see you doing something I don't like, you'll be out. But if you do the job well, in addition to being paid, you and the other servants will be able to have some of the leftover food."

"Thank you, sir."

"That's better."

He made leftover food sound wonderful. I didn't like the thought of eating food that the gentry didn't want, but I'd force myself.

Windbag was still speaking.

"Remember your place. You'll either be in the kitchen filling the platters or serving in The Great Hall. Don't let me see you wandering off into any of the other rooms. Is that clear? Go down to the kitchen now and ask cook – nicely, mind – to show you how to serve food to the gentry."

What a cheek! As though I'd want to see anything else! On the other hand, maybe I would have a quick look when this bossy butler wasn't looking.

The delicious smells of baking reached my nostrils before I had even entered the kitchen. Yes, it would be worth toadying to these people just to savour these lovely cakes.

"Are you one of the lads who's going to help serve the gentry on Saturday? Well, watch how I put these small pieces of food on the silver platters very neatly and show me how well you copy me. If you copy me exactly after trying twice, one of those honey cakes will be yours. Come on, now, you look like a capable boy."

This was easy. More like girls' work really. I did it just as cook wanted after the first try, so I got two cakes. I liked cook, and she certainly did bake delicious cakes. I'd like some more of those, so I supposed I'd better do as the butler and her were telling me. Were those plates really silver? I'd never seen silver before. Mouth-watering cakes and silver plates. Maybe I could begin to like how these people lived. It looked as though mother was right – again.

Chapter 8

My turned-up collar, plain necktie, crisp, white shirt, plain, dark-coloured waistcoat and long trousers looked very smart and fitted perfectly. Although my shoes were old, I'd put lots of dubbin on them so even they looked smart. In spite of being only 15, I was tall for my age and I knew, from the way the girls looked at me, that they must like what they saw. Wish we had a mirror so that I could see all of myself because I was sure I must look very smart. Even the river would only show bits of me. I put back my shoulders and stood straight. Funny how you can be the same person inside, but the outside is what others see and judge us on. Suddenly, my spirits lifted. Perhaps I might enjoy this after all.

In the kitchen, I joined several other boys and girls, some of whom I knew from the village. We were told we would be responsible for six silver platters each; the adult manservants were pouring the champagne. I wanted to do a good job for cook – and not just because of the reward - so I took my time arranging all the sweetmeats, which is what cook had put me in charge of. I had never seen so many different kinds. Cook told me it was gingerbread, sugared almonds and, best of all, tiny horses made of marzipan. I loved those! They all looked mouth-watering. So much so, in fact, that, once again, I changed my mind and hoped that some of these *would* be left by the gentry!

"Now, just be sure that all this food is put on the plates and taken into the Great Hall for the visitors. If I see any of you putting any of it into your pockets, you won't be given any that are left over later. You might not have a job, either. Do you hear?"

We all spoke together -

"Yes, cook."

I wasn't the only one who liked this small, rosy-cheeked woman who looked as though she enjoyed lots of her own cakes, too.

When all the platters had been filled, she waddled over and inspected them, neatening the occasional one, but, mainly saying, "Well done," with such a lovely smile that we all felt we'd done a very good job.

We then lined up and walked into the Great Hall, one behind the other. What sights, sounds and smells met our eyes, ears and noses! I couldn't believe how big the room was. Four or more of our cottages could fit into this one room – and there were obviously others, through doors that were closed. In spite of what I had said to mother, I longed to explore. I'd have to watch for my chance. At one end of the room were three people playing instruments. I thought one was a lute and Cook said the other was a virginal. And, although dancing didn't interest me, the Great Hall had become so lively with different types of dances that I couldn't help but want to join in. By now, even I knew that that wasn't possible, though.

A lady in a long, pretty dress was singing. The musicians were playing softly and, I noticed, as the numbers of people grew, they played gradually more loudly so that they could always be heard. It was a beautiful sound, and one I'd never heard before. I loved walking in the woods, listening to the songs of birds such as cuckoos and nightingales. Some of this music sounded like bird song. I also enjoyed sitting by the stream – even though it stank – as its bubbling and tumbling over the weirs was such a sweet sound. I loved dancing to the village fiddlers, too. But these three people were creating such lovely music that I wondered where it came from and how they did it. I would ask somebody later.

"Don't drop that, you silly boy! Keep your wits about you!"

The man's aggressive voice made me jump so much I almost did drop the food. And that would have been his fault, not mine. But guess who would have been blamed? And guess who wouldn't have been allowed to have a tasty cake after all? There were parts of this job I liked and parts I definitely didn't.

As I tightened my grip on the platter, it was at that very moment I knew. One day, some time, somehow, I would be a member of the gentry, and I would make young boys jump, too. But only if they were gentry. I would always try to treat my own kind as I wanted to be treated today. With respect and kindness. But mainly, the people I would command would be the gentry. Then they'd be sorry.

Chapter 9

Now that he was back at The Manor and in charge of it, Arthur recalled exactly how he had felt that very first time he had helped to serve here. He had been a servant serving the gentry. He remembered promising himself that he would always try to show respect to his servant colleagues but wouldn't care at all how he spoke to or treated the gentry. He couldn't help the household he had been born into any more than they could. So why should they think they were better than him?

He'd speak to Margory's maid himself the following day, telling her that her job was safe and that he liked servant girls. She looked nice enough. Might even like a kiss or two. Or more. He'd have to see whether he liked her. If he did, he might have to remind her that he was Lord of the Manor, of course. But that was fine. She was only a girl, after all. But never mind ingratiating himself with the servants. That could come later. What he had to do now was to ensure that Margory knew who was master here. Strange how the world turned. It didn't seem long since she had tried to command him. That was about to change. He'd make sure of that.

Chapter 10

"Tomorrow, I shall ensure that your friend – was Hugh his name? – knows that you are my wife and that I am the Lord of the manor. I shall make it perfectly clear that he is not welcome here. Oh, I saw how your face changed when you looked at him. Have you asked for forgiveness in your prayers for thinking about one man while still married to another? I couldn't care less about prayers, but I know you do." Margory stared at him.

"For all I knew, Arthur, you were dead. You have certainly been dead to me for four years. May I remind you that, when I really needed you after my parents were put to the stake, you informed me that you had taken all my family's money. Money that was earned by my grandfather as well as my father. You left me with nothing but a broken heart. But I have worked hard to mend my heart and have succeeded, with the help of loyal servants and friends of my parents."

"Aren't you forgetting someone who has clearly helped to mend your breakage? Your friend, Hugh. Or is he more than a friend? Is he also your lover?"

"How dare you suggest that a man as good as Hugh …"

"Oh, he's a good man, is he? Well, we'll see about that. We'll see what a good woman he thinks you are when he finds out that you still love me."

"Love you! I haven't loved you for several years, Arthur. You turned my heart to stone when you left. You made it clear how selfish a person you are when you told me that you had defrauded my dear father and bought a property elsewhere in the country. Then when you told me that poor Hannah was with child – your child – when she died, I turned my back on you and never wished to see you again. More's the pity that my wish didn't come true. I shall retire now, Arthur, as I'm very tired. I look forward to hearing your plans in the morning."

"You will hear more of my plans before the morrow, wife."

Chapter 11

"Turn to face me, wife. And don't ever turn your back on me again. I'll show you who's in command here. I said, turn to face me. As you told me you had turned your back on me when I left several years ago, now is your opportunity to gaze on my face. Do you remember when you wanted to gaze upon my face so very much?"

"What? What are you doing? Don't touch me! Get out of my bed! Don't ever touch me again. I do not wish it!"

The air only hung heavily for a matter of seconds. But the storm that then erupted was like nothing Margory had ever experienced.

"You do not WISH it! You will wish that those words had not left your lips by the time I have finished with you."

Margory summoned the little energy she had in trying to slide out of bed. She failed. Arthur forced one hand over her mouth, pressing her neck with the other. She tried to fight with all her might. But it was no good. As he continued to press her neck, her body lost its strength, becoming floppy.

"Your bed! This is our conjugal bed. You taught me words such as that. You taught me reading, writing and arithmetic when all you wanted was to marry me and have my children. I don't recall your telling me then to get out of your bed. This Hugh really has been worming his way into your affections, hasn't he. Does he know how you manipulated me into your life and tore Hannah – dear, pretty Hannah – out of it? Kitchen chatter said that when the soap slithered out of your hand when you were bathing, it wasn't an accident. Kitchen chatter said that when you insisted on Hannah – poor, ill Hannah – being taken to one of your guest bedrooms, that you were ensuring that I didn't visit her. I never wanted you. Why would I? You're plain, which is why none of the gentry wanted you. All I ever wanted, once it was clear that you and your revealing dresses and sucking of plums were heading for intimacy, was to lie with you in the woods – perhaps once. But that wasn't enough for you. Oh no, much to my amazement, you said we had to be churched because of our touching. So in spite of my mother's warning of no good coming of the mixing of classes, I saw an opportunity to climb even higher on society's ladder. That was the beginning of my wondering whether you were a witch. There had been other signs, after all. Otherwise, why would I have capitulated? I didn't even like you. But enough of that. Lie still you stupid woman. Be grateful."

Margory's breathing was becoming heavier as Arthur squeezed her neck even more. Trying to tear his fingers away from her mouth, she gasped,

"Stop touching me! Get dressed. I don't want you anywhere near me. Don't you understand? I shall scream."

"Oh, I don't think so. Some of your servants will probably remember that I didn't exactly rush to your bed when we lived together. So now that I'm in your bedroom, what will they think if you scream. I wouldn't want them to think you don't want babies with your husband. Because that's the word I would have to spread. I know you don't want that, so I'll just have to put my hand over your mouth. Think about it. It will stop the whispering. You have two choices: either lie back and enjoy the inevitable or resist. I have to say, a fighting woman is much more entertaining."

Margory did neither. Suddenly she could smell the semen. She could feel the sweat. Arthur's sweat. She could feel him ripping through her. She thought she would tear in two. Then, when she wanted to die, he relaxed and she felt the liquid running down her legs. All that was left of her was a body of sobbing. Even when she curled into herself, the pain was excruciating. She lay there, not moving.

"Well, if you'd given in, it wouldn't have hurt so much. What a shame. Next time, just pretend to like it. You fought like a cat. I didn't know you had it in you. I shall have to encourage that next time as I rather liked it. None of my other women have done that. It was your own fault."

Next time. How could she carry on living and risk a 'next time'? But continue living she must. But now that she had been defiled, who would want her? Certainly not Hugh. He was such a good man. How could he begin to believe that anyone would do such a thing. No, he would think that she was once again Arthur's wife in every way. She would never see him again. She must become accustomed to the withdrawal of his friendship that had begun the moment Arthur had entered her body.

Chapter 12

Margory lay in bed for days, not moving. Her maids came and her maids left, not understanding why their mistress was the embodiment of distress. All she did was to lie perfectly still, curled like a cat, sobbing as though her heart would break. Kitchen talk spoke of nothing else. Why wasn't Mistress Margory getting up? Why wasn't she bathing? And what was that pungent smell in her bedchamber that seemed to penetrate even the walls and bed hangings? What had happened to cause this change in her? What had upset her so horribly?

They hadn't seen Master Arthur for several days either, but Lucy, who some of them knew from several years before, was quietly helping wherever she was needed. When asked if she knew where Master Arthur was and why the mistress wasn't leaving her bed, she just shook her head, saying that she didn't know and didn't want to know. That she was content to not see Master Arthur. She then changed the subject.

On the third day of Margory's interminable sorrow, Hugh had arrived unannounced, asking for Goodwife Sykes. When he had asked to see the mistress, Goodwife Sykes had tried to turn him away, telling him that the mistress had taken to her bed, no-one knew why as she hadn't spoken. Hugh had then asked as to the whereabouts of Master Arthur, to which Goodwife Sykes couldn't reply. He had said he would wait for an hour and would Goodwife Sykes let her mistress know that he was in the library. The housekeeper had shaken her head but said that she would tell one of the maids to serve him a small ale and that she would go to her mistress to tell her that he would like to speak to her. Shortly afterwards, Goodwife Sykes had returned to tell him that, although she had told her mistress of his arrival, Mistress Margory had neither responded nor moved. Indeed, she told him, she hadn't moved for several days, it was not known why.

"Has the family physician been called?" Hugh had asked, full of concern.

"I'm afraid I don't have the authority to do that, sir, and no-one knows where Master Arthur is, whether he will return or when."

"Well, in that case, I shall speak to my employer, Lord Winchester, about this as it appears that your mistress is ill and nothing is being done about it. This isn't your fault, Goodwife Sykes, but I can't stand by and do nothing. Please ask for my horse to be brought to the front…"

The great door banged open and Arthur strode in.

"What pray is the reason for your presence? What is going on here? Is my wife entertaining you behind my back yet again?"

"Indeed she is not, sir. I understand that she is ill and hasn't left her bedchamber…"

"*Our* bedchamber."

"I see. Whatever the situation is between Margory and yourself, I am told that she hasn't left the bedchamber for several days. So it appears that something is amiss. Do you know what it is that ails the lady?"

"No, I don't. But what I do know is that it is not your concern. The lady is my wife and if she has taken to her bed, I shall be the one who makes sure she returns to her duties of running the household. Indeed, I shall ensure that happens if I have to drag her out of bed myself. Now, I suggest that you leave and I see no reason for your return. Is that clear?"

"My friendship with Mistress Margory…"

"Is at an end. Whatever may have existed between you and my wife is dead and buried now that I have returned to resume my rightful place at The Manor. And it looks as though my return has come at a fortuitous time. I'm sure you will agree that it is highly inappropriate for a vulnerable woman living on her own to have the type of friendship it appears was growing between the two of you."

"Our friendship always has been entirely innocent in nature but warm, as Margory has always been aware of her marital status and has never tried to hide it from me."

"In that case, you should be ashamed of yourself. Interesting that my wife should claim you to be a "good man" when you admit to toying with a woman who has given herself to another in church. Also, I've only got the word of the two of you that your relationship has been 'entirely innocent'..."

"How dare you suggest that we may not be telling the truth."

"I suggest you leave now, as there is no 'we' that assumes you have a relationship, of whatever kind, with my wife. Is that clear? You are no longer welcome in this house."

"I shall leave the moment you assure me that your family physician will be summoned to help your wife."

"That is no concern of yours. I shall make sure that my wife gets out of her bed, whether she wishes it or not. She has a husband and a household to organise and a wife who remains in bed for days at a time is of no use to me."

"But Margory..."

"Are you still here? I have asked you in a civil way to leave. If you do not do so immediately, I shall be obliged to have you thrown out. Yes, you may gasp, Goodwife Sykes, but this gentleman – if a gentleman he is – does not seem to realise that he is not welcome here. And if it appears that you have encouraged his visits, I shall throw you out, too, while making sure that no-one in the county employs you again."

"Now look here. Goodwife Sykes is a good woman... Yes, I shall leave now, but I shall not promise that I won't return."

"You'll be sorry if you do. I have friends who would be happy to do my bidding, while earning shillings for ale. If you return, you won't walk or ride again. I suggest that you stay away. In fact, I order you never to return. I repeat - you'll be sorry if you do. Do I make myself clear?"

Arthur's memory flew back to the day at Margory's Confirmation when he had vowed never to be commanded by gentry. This was one such moment.

Chapter 13

I was back among the gentry, listening to the music again at my wife's Confirmation so many years ago. I was walking among the silks and velvets of the ladies, hearing sometimes their talk of balls, needlework and drawing. I had noticed how some of them stood in small groups, their hands partly over their mouths, glancing at the male gentry and giggling. I remember wondering what they were saying. Probably silly girl talk again!

It was after I had re-filled my platter for the third time, receiving a pat on the back from cook, that I noticed a lady standing on her own. She didn't seem to be much older than me – perhaps a year – and she didn't look very happy. She was wearing a very pretty dress, so she must be a member of the gentry, but why wasn't she talking to anybody?

Next time I saw one of the other servants, I had whispered,

"Who's that lady?"

"Where?"

"Standing near the long table of food, in the pale blue dress?" I tried to point without dropping the platter.

"Don't you know who that is, silly? She's the reason for this party. It's Lord and Lady Francis's daughter, Mistress Margory."

"Well, if it's her party, why isn't she joining in, and why does she look so unhappy?"

"Don't tell anybody I said this, will you?"

"No, 'course not. What?"

"Promise?"

"Get on with it or I'm off to the kitchen."

"Well, you can see for yourself anyway. Her face is plain and she isn't thin, is she? It's said her plates are always piled high with food. Maybe that's why none of the other ladies and gentlemen talk to her very much. All they do is say a few polite words and move on. One of my friends said that if her father wasn't Lord of the Manor, they probably wouldn't speak to her at all."

"Mmm. See what you mean. Still, she's very rich, isn't she, so one of these members of the gentry could decide to put up with her, as long as he can buy whatever he wants. Anyway, whoever marries her wouldn't have to stay at home looking at her all the time, would he? He could be out with whichever pretty lady he wants."

"That's true. Er…I mean, what a nasty thing to say, Arthur. It is Arthur, isn't it? Oh look. A young lady who looks a bit like Mistress Margory has gone to speak to her. I'm not sure, but someone said she's the mistress's cousin and has come all the way from Essex. I think they said her name's Elizabeth Francis. It's also said that her sister is Agnes Waterhouse who has been known to dabble in witchcraft. But please don't tell anyone, anyone at all that I said that, will you?"

"Yes, well, I'm not interested in who's speaking to who. I'm off to the kitchen to see if there's anything else to eat." What I didn't say, though, was that I was intrigued by the mention of witchcraft. If Mistress Margory's relatives were witches, maybe she was one, too. Naah! Couldn't be. Otherwise she'd change her face. Even so, maybe I'd keep an eye out for anything witchy.

"Come on, you two. Stop your chattering. Not gossiping about your betters, are you?"

It was the grumpy butler again.

"Just going back to cook for a refill – er – sir."

Chapter 14

In the fields the next day, I had told my friends, mainly Simon, all about the party. The more I had told them, the more I liked the way they were looking at me admiringly.

"Yes, you should have seen the room where it was going on. You could fit all the village into just that room. I looked in every room in the house…"

"You never!"

"Yes, I did. And they were all huge. Every one I went into was bigger than the one I'd just left. First I looked everywhere downstairs, then I went up this very grand staircase…"

"You never!"

"Up there were all the chambers where they sleep. Although there's only the Lord and Lady and their daughter – who told me her name was Margory…"

"She never spoke to you!"

"Oh yes. I could see she thought I was handsome…"

"Yuk. Never mind her. What else did you see?"

"There was 100 rooms…"

"Naw. Not 100."

"Well, maybe 90. Anyway, what does it matter? There was room after room after room. When I went into each chamber, it had a fireplace, glazed windows and a four poster bed. There were diamonds, rubies and pearls on some of the dressing tables. I've never seen anything like it. And then there was the food. I got to eat some of that as well…"

"You never!"

"Is that all you can say? I tell you, I couldn't believe my eyes. There were cakes – as many as I could eat…"

"Could have took some for us."

"Yes, well. Next time…"

"Next time? What do you mean, 'next time'? Are you going in there again?"

"'Course I am. And when I do, I'll bring you your favourite sweetmeat. Just see if I don't."

Suddenly I was aware of Master Green, the Foreman.

"What're you lads chattering about? Get on with your work. If I see you talking instead of working again, you'll get the back of my hand. What will Mistress Margory think?"

I had been so absorbed in my story, I didn't know what he meant. But then I noticed Mistress Margory who was seated on the most beautiful horse I'd ever seen. It was a gorgeous chestnut colour, with slender limbs and flowing mane. Its eyes were so big I thought it was looking right through me. Certainly the Mistress was looking straight at me. She didn't say anything, she just looked. How long had she been there? I started to walk towards the horse but was hauled back by the scruff of the neck and dragged away.

"And where do you think you're going m'lad? What did I tell you? Did my eyes deceive me, or were you going to speak to Mistress Margory, daughter of the Lord of The Manor? You, who's nothing but a servant and always will be."

He hit me so hard across the back of my legs that I jumped, but I didn't cry or anything. I didn't even shout out. I wouldn't show him that it had hurt, but it had. When I looked at my legs, they were bright red and burning. I was embarrassed that Mistress Margory had seen what happened, but when I turned to look at her and her horse again, they were nowhere to be seen. I'd never forgive him for that. Making me look silly in front of the daughter of the Lord of The Manor. No, I wouldn't forget it, either.

Chapter 15

"Have you had a good day, Arthur?"

"All right, I s'pose. Saw a beautiful horse, with Mistress Margory riding it. I want a horse like that some day, mother."

"Yes, well, it's all right to dream, just so long as you understand that that's all it is – a dream. As you like horses so much, maybe you could think about doing an apprenticeship as a stable hand for his Lordship eventually. However, at the moment, I'm feeling more tired every day as this little scrap jumps, bumps and kicks in my belly, so I'd like your help with the washing before you start wishing yourself on a fine horse. When we're at church, you could ask God what He thinks about your working for the Lord of The Manor."

Truth was, Arthur only went to church with the family because that's what everybody did, and because everybody had to, but he wasn't sure why he went. Maybe he would try praying for a horse and see what happened. He'd been told that nearly everybody prayed for either a horse or money. In the meantime, he couldn't stop dreaming about how very much he wanted a lot of money so that he could buy whatever he wanted, when he wanted it. He would, he thought, start with several stables of fine horses; he would eat pheasant and goose and fresh river eels every day, and as many cakes as he wanted. He'd never look at brown bread again, with all its bits that ground into your teeth. He promised himself that everybody in the County of Hertfordshire would know that he was very important because of his expensive clothes. And, if any of the gentry said something to him that he didn't like – well, he wasn't sure what he would do, but it wouldn't be nice. His mother's voice pierced his dream. She always managed to bring him back to earth, with a thud.

"Arthur! Stop your day-dreaming and help me with this washing – now!"

Oh yes, and he would make sure that his mother never had to wash and cook again because she'd have dozens of servants to do that for her. He just had to decide how he was going to get all that money.

"Yes, mother."

Chapter 16

"Are you Arthur Wright?"

"Yes, who are you?"

"Never you mind. I work at The Manor for his Lordship, is all you need to know. Come with me."

"What for?"

"Got a real little tongue on you, haven't you. I said, you're coming with me."

By then, the man in charge in the fields as well as Arthur's father, Simon and a few of his other friends had gathered, wondering what was going on. His father asked,

"What d'you want with my son, eh?"

"This little thief's yours, is he? I wouldn't be so proud of him, if I were you. Lord at The Manor wants to see him. Word's got back that he might know something about some missing jewellery."

"What! My son's no thief, leave 'im be."

"We'll see about that. If the Lord agrees with you, he'll be back in the fields quick as a wink."

Arthur's father began to shake him.

"What you done, lad? Tell me straight. You don't usually lie, so don't start now. When I'm at the ale house earning a bit more money, I don't want everyone telling me I've got a thief for a son."

"Don't know what he's talking about, father. Honest."

Simon whispered in his ear,

"Yesterday you said you went all over the house. Did you see anybody else who might've taken this jewellery stuff?"

Arthur shuffled his feet and looked down at the crops growing in the field, feeling his cheeks growing warm.

"What're you two whispering about. Don't look good to me. This lad looks very shifty. Pity your poor mother if she's brought up a thief for a son. She's a good woman, that one. Or maybe you're turning out to be just like your father – a lazy drinker. Come on, his Lordship's waiting."

At the mention of his mother, Arthur felt a solitary tear running down his cheek. He brushed it away with his sleeve, feeling annoyed. He knew, of course, that the only two rooms he had gone into at The Manor were the kitchen and the Great Hall. But in his excitement, he had boasted to his friends, mainly Simon, that he went all over the house. He was a bit puzzled because he knew that Simon wouldn't have said anything to anybody. And now he'd have to tell the truth, with no extra bits.

His Lordship's manservant dragged Arthur over the fields and in through the servants' door.

"Now, lad. If you've done nothing wrong, you've got nothing to fear. His Lordship's a fair man and he'll listen to what you have to say. But if you have, you'll be punished, good and proper. And quite right, too."

"Done nothing."

"Hope not, for your sake. Straighten your jerkin, stand up straight and answer all his Lordship's questions truthfully. All right?"

"Yes, sir."

"That's better. Glad to hear you keeping that tongue of yours in check. Now, in we go. His Lordship's been waiting long enough in his study."

Chapter 17

In spite of his shaking knees, Arthur put back his shoulders and followed the manservant into the study where, not only was the Lord seated behind a desk, but his daughter was in a chair nearby. Arthur looked at them both quickly and lowered his eyes. But before doing so, he noticed that the Lord's daughter was looking at him quite intently, yet again, and he wondered why. In turn, that made him momentarily think about her having stopped her horse when he was in the fields the day before. His Lordship brought Arthur back to the present.

"Come on in, lad. Arthur, isn't it? I'm Lord Francis and this is my daughter, Mistress Margory. I'll get straight to the point. You were one of the servants who helped at my daughter's Confirmation celebration, were you not?"

"Yes, sir, I mean, your Lordship, I was."

"Don't worry. 'Sir' is fine. Both show that you've been brought up to be respectful."

"Yes, sir, my mother likes me to be respectful."

"Well, I'm very glad to hear you say that, Arthur. Did you enjoy helping at the celebration?"

Arthur began to relax a little as his Lordship sounded friendly.

"Oh yes, sir. I enjoyed it a lot. Particularly as cook is so nice and we got to have some of her sweetmeats when we did things proper-like."

His Lordship smiled.

"So. You like sweetmeats, do you. Well, if you tell the truth today, you'll be rewarded with more of them, and some to take to your mother, too. Would you like that?"

"Oh yes, sir. With her Ladyship's help, my mother is having another little'un soon, so she'd like that very much."

"Oh, is she? She's a lucky lady. Right, well, let's get on. Remember, I only want to hear the truth."

"Yes, sir."

"Well, Arthur, tell me which rooms you went into at the celebration."

Arthur hesitated. His boasting was about to be found out.

"First, I went into the kitchen."

"And what did you do in the kitchen?"

"Cook gave us all jobs to do, Sir, er, your Lordship. Mine was to put these little sweetmeats on to platters. She said that when each was empty, I was to go back and fill it up again. I filled six platters which meant that cook was pleased and gave me some cakes as a reward."

"And which other room did you go into?"

"Begging your pardon, sir, but the Great Hall, of course, which is where I took the platters around for the gentry."

"Of course. And which other rooms did you go into? This is an important question, Arthur, so think carefully."

Again, Arthur hesitated.

"Perhaps you went to the jakes, did you? That would be fine, Arthur, and you can tell me if that was the case."

"No, sir, I didn't. I wanted to, at the end, but I didn't know where it was and, besides, I was too busy, so I waited until I got back home."

"So you only went into two rooms, Arthur – the kitchen and the Great Hall. Is that right?"

"It is, sir."

"Why is it then, Arthur, that word has got back to me that you went all over the house? Is that just idle chatter, or are you not telling me the truth? Think carefully before you answer, Arthur. I want your mother to be proud of you."

Arthur swallowed. Both Lord Francis and Mistress Margory were looking at him very closely. He knew his mother was proud of him. But she didn't know about his boasting the day before. He wondered who'd been whispering about him behind his back. It didn't matter, though, as it was his own fault. He shouldn't have said he'd been in places he hadn't. Now, his exaggerating had come back to bite him where it hurt. Arthur decided he had better be honest.

"Begging your pardon, sir. I was telling the truth to you just now when I said I only went into two rooms – the kitchen and Great Hall. I s'pose I'd better tell you, though, that, yesterday, I was so excited to have been picked to come into The Manor that I boasted to my friends about what I'd seen. I said that I'd been everywhere here when, in fact, I hadn't at all. I didn't have time, sir, as I was so busy. I'm really very sorry about what I said to my friends, and I'll be careful not to do that again."

"That would be very wise of you, Arthur, because, you see, some jewellery belonging to my daughter was stolen, we think during the celebration. When we heard that you said you had gone everywhere in the house, I had to make sure that it wasn't you. Do you understand that your boasting could have got you into very serious trouble? Boys younger than you have been hung for stealing."

Arthur gulped.

"Yes, I do, sir. Please, sir, will you have to tell my mother and father?"

"Yes, I'm afraid I shall, Arthur. But I shall also tell them that I sincerely believe you have told me the truth, which was brave of you. I shall say that I don't think you will boast again in that way, and that I shall be very disappointed if they mete out any punishment. In fact, what I think I shall do is speak to Lady Francis and ask her to have a quiet word with your mother when she visits her next time."

"Thank you very much, sir. I would like that, as my mother could then tell my father when it's a good time."

"Quite so." His Lordship smiled and winked at me.

Arthur decided he liked him. That liking made him bolder.

"I know it's nothing to do with me, sir, but may I ask a question?"

"Of course."

"As I wasn't the person who stole Mistress Margory's jewels, there is someone out there who did, and I wonder what you're going to do next about it?"

"Well, that's a good question, Arthur, and one to which I shall have to give some thought. As you say, it now has nothing to do with you, and I am very pleased with the way you have behaved today. Giles. Take this young man to cook and tell her he is allowed to choose his favourite sweetmeats, some of which are to be taken to his mother."

Chapter 18

Still, I remember wondering at the time who had really stolen Mistress Margory's jewels and who'd repeated that I'd gone through the Manor House. It must have been somebody who was standing nearby when I was telling my friend, Simon. Somebody didn't like me, and did that somebody know who had really stolen the jewels? Back in the fields, I'd found myself looking at the other boys differently. I thought there must be somebody there I really didn't know at all. I decided I would watch out.

Later, when I went home, Lady Francis was with my mother. Mistress Margory was also there, and looked up as I walked in. Again, I found her staring at me long and hard. Why did she do that?

"Everything is absolutely fine, Goodwife Wright. Nothing to worry about at all. Just let me know if you're at all concerned about anything. Also, I suggest that my daughter, Mistress Margory, plays a bigger part in your delivery than she has done in deliveries in the past. She has, of course, been accompanying me since she was eight years old, so has a lot of knowledge and experience already. She also loves it. I know she is going to be an excellent midwife on her own estate some day."

Then I heard my mother say,

"I would be delighted to have your daughter's help, Lady Francis. I wonder if I may raise a subject, too, that my eldest child, Arthur, and I've been discussing lately. Although he can't read nor write, he's an intelligent boy, and I would like to see him go further than simply working in the fields, important though that is. He was so taken with The Manor that I was wondering if there might be a position of some sort there. Perhaps with the horses, or one of the servant's positions in The Manor itself."

Looking at me, Lady Francis had said,

"I'm very pleased to hear you say that Arthur would like to progress in his work, Goodwife Wright. I can tell you now that my husband was impressed when he spoke to him a few days ago. I shall tell Lord Francis what you have said, as he knows much more about the running of the estate than I do, of course, and is in a better position to know what may be possible." Turning to me, she then asked,

"Do you think that you would be happy working for Lord Francis, Arthur? Of course, you wouldn't be working directly for him, but for someone else."

My face had lit up with pleasure.

"Oh yes, your Ladyship. I would like that very much. Although I would like to work directly for Lord Francis some time in the future, if that became possible."

"Yes well, Lord Francis would need to think about that, as I'm sure you realise, Arthur. There will, of course, be a great deal for you to learn first. I shall let your mother know what my husband says next time I visit. In the meantime, I'm sure you do a very good job in the fields, and we would want to hear first how well you are getting on there before you are offered another position."

"Thank you, Lady Francis."

Then, turning to her daughter, I asked,

"Will you be riding your beautiful horse near the fields again, Mistress Margory?" Mother was quick in her rebuke.

"Arthur! That's an impertinent question. Watch your tongue!"

But Mistress Margory was smiling,

"I'm sure he meant no offence, Goodwife Wright. And yes, I may well be riding by in the next few days."

I was pleased. I did so love to see beautiful horses.

Chapter 19

I clearly remembered the first thing I'd noticed - her riding boots. I thought they might be deer skin, and the tops were turned down to reveal a bright red lining. They had buttons, an elegant, small heel and I supposed they were very fashionable. Ladies always seemed to be keen on dressing fashionably. I had tried to stand in such a way that the holes in my shoes didn't show very much but it wasn't easy and I nearly fell over. That had made me feel a bit silly and I knew my face was going pink.

"Hello Arthur! I'm glad to see you again. Are you all right? Is your leg hurting? You seem to be standing strangely. No, he's not troubling me, Master Green. He'll be back to work any moment now."

"Do you ride, Arthur?"

"Oh yes, I do, Mistress Margory, but my horse is quite old, so I don't do it as often as I'd like."

"Well, I'm sure we can do something about that. Enjoy your work in the fields, Arthur. Goodbye for now."

That had been a narrow escape; I didn't think she'd seen my shoes.

At home, that evening, I had sat by the fire wondering what Mistress Margory had meant. She certainly was friendly towards me. Mother had finished her spinning and asked,

"You're quiet this evening, Arthur. Anything wrong?"

"Doesn't matter."

I knew what I had to do next.

"I may be a little late home tomorrow evening, mother."

"Oh, why's that?"

"I'll tell you when I'm back."

"No mischief, mind. It was bad enough when Lord Francis was told that you might have stolen Mistress Margory's jewels. Has the thief been found yet?"

"Don't think so. Haven't heard."

"Well, just you make sure that you don't start exaggerating again."

"Oh, I shall, mother. When is Lady Francis coming again about the new baby?"

"Not for another two weeks. Why?"

"Oh, just wondered."

Chapter 20

I remember forcing my face into a smile as the butler opened the door. Didn't want him to see that I was nervous.

"Oh, it's you again. What do you want?"

"Want to speak to Lord Francis."

"Oh, you do, do you? And what may I ask do you want to speak to his

Lordship about? And will he want to speak to you, you ragamuffin? You shouldn't be at this door. There's a door round the back for the likes of you."

I'd bitten my lip. Better not to aggravate this man, or anyone else who worked for His Lordship, for that matter."

"Want to speak to him about working here instead of the fields."

"Oh, do you indeed. Well, you'd better go to the servants' door while I'm finding his Lordship's manservant. I'll tell him to see you there. We still haven't found who was responsible for taking Mistress Margory's jewels and until we do, you'd better be extra careful."

"Yes, sir."

I looked down, pretending to look humble, but all the time I was thinking that one day this man would be somebody else who'd be sorry. Seemed silly to have to go to another door when I was already in the house. Another stupid gentry rule.

He was gone so long I thought he was never coming back and was wondering whether I should just leave, when the door opened. I looked up to see quite an old man looking down at me, smiling very kindly.

"Come this way, lad. Arthur isn't it? His Lordship told me about you. There's a room off one of the kitchens where we can be private. If you smile nicely at cook on the way through, she might give you a couple of her biscuits that I could smell baking this morning."

And he winked at me. Winked! I decided that, as well as cook, I liked this man, too. Perhaps not everybody was bad at The Manor after all. Although I intended to make a lot of money and become a member of the gentry one day, I was beginning to feel a bit muddled about how I felt about class. Were gentry bad and servants, good. Maybe as I got a little older I would know the answer.

Lowering himself slowly into a chair, the old man said,

"Now, lad, what can I do for you? I'm Master Stephen, his Lordship's main manservant. I've worked for him since long before you were born, so there isn't much I don't know about The Manor. First of all, how old are you?"

"15, sir."

"And how long have you been working in the fields?"

"Not sure, Sir. Seems a long time. What I do know is that I would like to become an apprentice here, at the Manor House, not in fields. As I love horses, perhaps in the stables."

"Don't you like it in the fields, then?"

"Oh, I do like some things. I've got a lot of friends in the fields; I like working outside, and my father has always worked there. But it's a bit boring, and I don't want to work there forever. I'd like to be able to get a bigger cottage for my parents and buy them better clothes. And a fine horse, and…"

"Whoa, lad. That's enough to start off with. So you're ambitious, are you?"

"If 'ambitious' means having nice clothes, delicious food and a better place to live, then, yes, I s'pose I am ambitious, as you call it. I like horses a lot, too."

"Well, nothing wrong with that, lad. Just so happens I'm beginning to need somebody to help me do everything for

His Lordship 'cos I'm not as young as I was. Old bones are beginning to creak a bit these days. Can't bend and lift like I used to so maybe I could teach you what I do. What do you think? Would you like that, Arthur?"

"Oh yes, sir, I'd like that a lot."

"Good. Well, you leave that to me because his Lordship will have to give his approval, of course."

"When Lady Francis visited my mother last time, she said she'd speak to his Lordship about it, but I know that she's really busy, so thought I'd speak for myself."

"Good for you. His Lordship likes initiative – that means speaking up for yourself – so let's hear what he has to say. When I've spoken to him, I'll send one of the servants to your cottage to let you know."

I beamed as he turned and hobbled away slowly. I'd got a bit of a plan forming in my head. It was going well so far.

Chapter 21

"You did what?! Arthur, what am I going to do with you? Her Ladyship *said* that she would let us know when she had spoken to his Lordship. Some day your cheek is going to get you into trouble."

"Won't you be pleased when I buy you a new pair of shoes? Yours aren't much better than my galoshes. You should have seen the riding boots Mistress

Margory was wearing."

"You just don't understand, Arthur, do you. How often do I have to tell you? That's because she's gentry and we're not. Oh, and here comes her Ladyship now."

"Good evening, Goodwife Wright. I hope I find you well. Perhaps the children would like to sit in another part of the room while you and I chat in a moment. Well, Arthur. Lord Francis tells me that you decided to take matters into your own hands by coming to The Manor yesterday. I have to say that I was more than a little surprised as I thought I had made it clear that I would let you know myself, which is something I would not normally do.

However, his Lordship was quite amused, and has asked me to give you his message myself, which I agreed to do on this occasion. He would like you to come to The Manor tomorrow at 5 of the clock to speak to Master Stephen.

You are not to be late, is that clear? Those who are fortunate enough to be employed in our household know that His Lordship and I insist upon punctuality."

"Yes, your Ladyship."

"Also, I understand that you came to the great door of The Manor and asked to speak to his Lordship. I am uncertain as to why you would take that liberty, but we shall say it is because your manners are those of a field worker at the moment, in spite of the fact that I know your mother to be very polite."

Mother glanced at me and dipped her head.

"I am truly sorry, your Ladyship, for my son's behaviour. It won't happen again."

"I sincerely hope not, and I shall overlook it on this occasion. I believe that you were shown the servants' door, and it is there you should present yourself for the appointment with Master Stephen tomorrow."

"Yes, your Ladyship."

"Good. Now I must speak to your mother, so I suggest you and your sister play games over there. I assume your husband is at the inn, as usual, Goodwife Wright?"

She waved her hand in the direction of the corner of the room in dismissal. In fact, I decided to go to bed early and told my sister to do the same. In that way, I avoided mother's tongue until the morning.

Chapter 22

Just as I had thought. Mother had told me off in her own way,

"No break for you today, young man. Just come home quickly from the fields and put on your best jerkin. You know, the one your father has passed down to you. You heard what her Ladyship said – you mustn't be late. As you're wanting to work at The Manor so much, you must start as you mean to go on. I know you can work hard if you want to."

"Yes, mother."

"Don't come all meek and mild with me now, Arthur. Just because I haven't punished you for the behaviour that her Ladyship described yesterday doesn't mean I'm not very disappointed in you. You need to know that

I was extremely embarrassed by the description of your behaviour and you must not shame me like that again. Do you understand, Arthur?"

"Yes, mother. I'm sorry."

"To be perfectly honest, Arthur, I'm very surprised that his Lordship is agreeing to your working at The Manor at all as I haven't heard that a thief has been named yet for stealing Mistress Margory's jewels. It's a mystery, and until the culprit is found, I feel that there is a shadow hanging over your head and that of your whole family."

"Please don't say that, mother. I promise you I'd nothing at all to do with the theft. Also, I feel sure that if his Lordship thought I did it, he wouldn't consider me working at The Manor."

"Yes, perhaps you're right. Anyway, away with you to the fields. You're not working at The Manor yet, m'boy, and until you do, we need those earnings, meagre though they are."

Chapter 23

"Well, Arthur, you look very smart – and you were right on time for your appointment. Well done. I'm very pleased, and so will his Lordship be. That's a good start. Keep it up and you'll go far, m'lad."

That was what I wanted to hear. And I did intend to go far, as Master Stephen put it.

"I've been thinking what your duties might be, and I've discussed it with his Lordship, who agrees. What you will do is work part of the time with me, learning what I do, and partly with Thomas who is in charge of the stables. In that way, you'll learn about the workings of The Manor as well as the stables. For the years you'll be learning, you'll earn very little. I know you eat at home at the moment, of course. However, when you start working at the Manor you'll live in and eat here every day. You'll eat with the servants, naturally. Also, every three months I shall speak to you about how you're getting on. I shall tell you what you're doing well and what you're not doing so well. Thomas will do the same, and will keep me informed. Every six months I shall tell his Lordship how you're getting on. However, although you will earn very little, if you're doing well in the stables, at the end of the first six months you'll be given your own horse. It won't be the best horse, of course. I'm sure you realise that a mere servant such as yourself would not be given a good horse. But it will be good enough for your needs. Now, lad, I'd like you to talk to your parents about this arrangement to make sure that they agree with them. In the meantime, what do you think? These are exciting new doors opening for you. Be sure you deal with this opportunity sensibly."

Chapter 24

And that's how it had begun. It wasn't so much a matter of doors opening for me as my pushing open those doors myself. I didn't intend to be using the servants' door forever. But it would do for now.

My days began to fall into a routine of breaking my fast with the other servants seated at the far end of the long dining table that seemed to go on forever and ever in the Great Hall. Lord and Lady Francis and Mistress

Margory came to the other end of the table for the mid-day meal, but they were so far off that none of us could hear what they were saying. Without her beautiful horse, Mistress Margory was of no interest to me. However I did notice that she glanced in my direction lots of times. Although I wondered why, I remembered my mother's caution of politeness so I smiled at her, at which I saw that her face became all pink. It looked as though Lady

Francis had noticed this, too, as she immediately began to talk to her daughter, while glaring at me. But why was Lady Francis staring at me like that? I didn't understand. Women were a mystery to me. It just made me think that gentry were very strange people. Perhaps mother was right – she usually was – when she said that they were quite different from poor people like us.

So, having done my duty of politeness and smiled at Mistress Margory, I turned back to talk to the other servants. In particular, on my very first day, I was joined by a pretty young maid to my right.

"Hello. What's your name?, I asked her. My name's…"

"Oh, I know what your name is. Everybody does. How you came and knocked on the great door at the front of The Manor and asked to speak to his Lordship. You were very brave. I know I couldn't do something like that. My name's Hannah."

My chest puffed like a pigeon's.

"What a very pretty name and oh, it were nothing. If I hadn't been allowed in, I'd have gone to another estate."

"No! Would you really?"

Just then I remember being aware of mother's words in my ear about boasting, so I closed my mouth in case other words that weren't quite true should escape.

"Well no, probably not, just teasing. My family are tenants on Lord

Francis's land, my father has worked on this land all his life so this is the only place I want to work. Particularly now I know there are such pretty young girls as you here."

I looked at her as I spoke these last words and was delighted to see her large, blue eyes lower, so that the dark fringe of lashes brushed her flawless skin. I had a sudden rush of wanting to stroke my lips over that softness. I'd never felt that feeling before.

"Well, I still think you were very brave. My father died last year and my mother cleans here, but she isn't well, so I'm lucky to have this position at The

Manor. We're tenants, too. Some Lords of the Manor would have thrown us out when we weren't able to pay the rent, but not Lord Francis. He's a very kind man. "

"I'm sorry about your father. It must be hard for you and your mother, and yes, I like his Lordship, too. So what do you do here?"

"I'm one of Mistress Margory's maids. Florence – she nodded in her direction – is her main maid, but she's leaving, and I think the Mistress is going to ask me to take her place, but I hope she doesn't."

"Whyever not? That'd mean you'd be paid more and it'd be better work."

"Yes, you're right. You're new here so you'll find out. Mistress Margory is, well, not very easy to work for, shall we say, but if she asks me I shall have to agree."

"What d'you mean?"

"She's got a bad temper that can come on in a flash. It's quite frightening. For some reason, at those times she reminds me of a witch. If I tell you something, do you promise not to tell? I don't usually chatter about other people, but everyone else seems to here, so I don't suppose it matters, really."

I was just about to move closer as Hannah's voice had become a low whisper, but, on looking towards the other end of the table, I noticed that Mistress Margory was frowning at me, but turned away when she saw me looking. That was the first time I'd seen her frown and it struck me as odd. Perhaps she was unhappy about something to do with her parents' conversation. Anyway, it couldn't have anything to do with me.

"I promise."

"Double promise? Because if Mistress Margory hears about my telling you, she'll dismiss me, and there'll be plenty of other young maids ready to step into my job."

At the risk of another frown from the other end of the table, I did lean closer because this sounded quite exciting. I wanted to know more about the young Mistress of the Manor who rode a fine horse and wore beautiful boots.

"Well, all the servants know anyway, so it can't harm."

"Yes, go on then, spit it out."

I was due to go to the stables as soon as I'd finished this meal and I couldn't wait to start working with the horses.

"Remember that you were accused of stealing Mistress Margory's jewels?"

"How did you know that? And how could I forget?"

"Oh, everybody knows. Well, Florence says Mistress Margory had hidden them."

"What?"

I couldn't believe my ears. I leaned in closer, not wanting to miss anything.

"Yes, she tells Florence everything, and she told her she'd been riding by and heard you boasting to your friends that you'd been all over the house when she knew you hadn't. So she told Florence she was going to teach you a lesson and say that her jewels were missing so that you'd be suspected. It's very mysterious, isn't it? Why do you think Mistress Margory would do that?"

I was so utterly astonished that, for a moment, I couldn't say anything at all.

"Maybe she wanted me off her father's land. But I don't know why that would be. I've never done her any harm."

"That isn't the end of the story."

"That's enough for me. How could she have me accused like that, and why was I let off so lightly by his Lordship?"

"Florence also told me that when Mistress Margory heard that her father was going to speak to you himself, she was a bit worried. So just after you'd seen him, she told him that she'd found them, having only misplaced them. Florence said that the Mistress also told her father how she'd overheard your boasting in the field so had thought it must be you. His Lordship loves his family very much, so believed every word she said."

I was shocked. Mistress Margory's behaviour was very strange.

"I'll see you tomorrow to break our fast."

Hannah looked anxious.

"Don't forget what you promised."

"Oh, I won't, trust me."

Chapter 25

I'd rushed out to the stables, longing to see the horses. This was my favourite work. I'd been put in charge of 2 stallions, 3 mares and a two-and-a-half-year-old colt. I fed and watered them daily as well as cleaning out their stables and grooming them. I was delighted with all six, but in particular the colt, Magic. I really hoped that he would be the one I would be allocated, if all went well, in six months' time as he already stood at 14 hands and was very handsome.

While grooming and talking to one of the stallions, I was surprised to see

Mistress Margory in the yard as I thought the Head Groom, Thomas, usually took her horse to the front of The Manor. Again, I thought how smart she looked in her dark blue jacket and skirt. I intended to dress smartly one of these days. Oh no, she was coming over to speak to me.

"Hello, Arthur. How are you getting on? You seem to be enjoying working in the stables. Has any particular horse taken your eye? I told you you would have your own one of these days. And I was right, wasn't I?"

"Yes, Mistress."

Wish she would go away and leave me to the horses. I liked them more than her.

"Cat got your tongue? You couldn't stop talking the day I saw you in the fields."

I didn't like the way this conversation was going. Mother was known to do things like interpret dreams and was also interested in different words people said. Just so happened that the week before, she had told me that the saying, 'Cat got your tongue?' went back hundreds of years, when it was believed that if you saw a witch, her cat would somehow "steal" or control your tongue so you couldn't say you'd seen her. Also, why was she talking about my speaking to the lads in the field as I now knew that she had overheard what I had said. Mistress Margory certainly was mysterious and I thought I'd better be careful. Was she now going to say that I'd stolen a horse? I knew that laws had been passed under our queen to reduce horse theft because so many were being taken. I was really pleased that the pretty little servant, Hannah, seemed to be a simple, uncomplicated girl whereas I just didn't know what to make of Mistress Margory.

"Well?"

"Er, sorry Mistress Margory, what did you say?"

"Weren't you even listening to me! What a very rude boy you are. Oh, never mind. I think you'd better learn – and fast – Arthur, that when a member of the gentry talks to you, you are very fortunate. Why, after all, should we superior beings even glance in the direction of servants? I, for one, have better things to do with my time than look at you, a stable boy, never mind speak to you." And with that she galloped quickly out of the yard, her cloak flying behind her.

A smile punctured my puzzlement. She did, actually, look a bit like a witch.

On the other hand, I admired the way she sometimes rode her horses astride instead of side saddle. I decided that I'd need to be careful around her.

"Oh dear, Magic, you're much easier to deal with than Mistress Margory."

He whinnied and seemed to nod in agreement as I stroked his black, shiny coat tenderly.

Chapter 26

Although I particularly enjoyed my work in the stables and the friendship of the other stable lads, I was surprised how much I also liked seeing the girl servants when I was working in The Manor itself, just as mother had said I might. In particular, I found myself hoping that I would be sitting next to Hannah at meal times. I realised that I felt much more at ease when we were breaking our fast, as his Lordship's family ate later. That meant I could concentrate on talking to Hannah and the other girls without wondering whether Mistress Margory was watching me – at which times I continued to smile brightly, receiving a similar, though weaker response. I began to realise that if I hadn't smiled at her for some time, my smile would be acknowledged with a haughty, slight inclination of her head, before turning away. It was perplexing but I wasn't bothered.

One day, Stephen told me to fetch his Lordship's shoes and, when passing

Mistress Margory's bedchamber, I saw Hannah about to go in to dust.

"Has the Mistress said anything more to you about becoming her main

Maid? Florence will be leaving soon, won't she?"

"Yes, she told me this morning that she wants to speak to me about it tomorrow before I have my morning meal. That means I shall be late, so I won't be able to sit next to you. But I'm sure one of the other maids will be happy to take my place."

She said this rather sadly so, putting my forefinger under her chin, I raised her face to mine so that she had to look directly into my eyes.

"There's no one I would rather sit next to than you, Hannah. I want you to know that."

She then surprised me by giving me a quick, feather-like kiss on the cheek, before rushing off, just as Mistress Margory rounded the corner.

"What are you doing here, by my bedchamber, Arthur. Not looking for jewels again, are you? What were you and Hannah doing?"

"Not looking for jewels, Mistress Margory, and never was.

Master Stephen sent me on an errand to his Lordship's bedchamber and I happened to bump into Hannah."

At that, she said nothing, but went into her bedchamber, closing the door crisply behind her. What a strange person she was.

Chapter 27

"Have you heard?"

"What?"

"Mistress Margory told me yesterday that I'm to be her personal maid when she returns from Gloucester, but not before. She said that I'm not experienced enough to help her to go to the balls. I felt a bit sorry about that because it sounds so exciting."

"Well, I'm pleased that you're not going. How long will she be away?"

"Three months, she said."

"Three months! That's absolutely wonderful. Think of the walks we can take, Hannah. We can walk in the woods…"

"Oh, I don't think Mistress Margory would like that."

"What makes you think that? Has she said you're not to walk on my arm? Has she?"

"Well no, she hasn't exactly said I mustn't walk on your arm. Neither has she said we mustn't walk into the woods. Perhaps this sounds a little silly – and I am a little silly, as you know – but it's just a feeling I have that she wouldn't like it."

"I don't think you're silly, Hannah. I think you're lovely. But if Mistress Margory hasn't told you not to walk on my arm or into the woods, why shouldn't we?"

"You're so clever, Arthur. I wish I was as clever as you."

Arthur thought he was clever, too, but nobody expected girls to be clever.

"When is Mistress Margory leaving? Who will you be helping while she's gone?"

"In two days. Mistress has told me that I must help Lady Francis's other maids as well as cook or wherever I'm needed. She said I must work hard while she's gone and that she will ask me what I have done when she returns. I wish I could read and write because, if I could, I would write down what I shall be doing so that Mistress Margory won't think I've been lazy."

"Of course you won't be lazy, Hannah. If Mistress Margory returns and says you've been lazy, just tell her to speak to me!"

"Ooooh! Arthur, you're so brave. But I couldn't do that. Oh, I think that's Mistress Margory calling for me now. I do so love talking to you, my brave Arthur, but I must go now. Mistress doesn't like to be kept waiting."

Arthur felt such sorrow in his heart as he watched Hannah dash away, his heart leaping when she turned and blew him a kiss. What a dear, dear girl she was.

Chapter 28

Arthur could remember the day Margory had left as though it was yesterday. He must have looked around every corner in The Manor for Hannah, but she was nowhere to be found. Surely she hadn't forgotten that they were going to have three wonderful months together while Margory was away.

But no, there she was, later that afternoon, sitting in her usual place at the table.

"Hannah. I've been looking everywhere for you. It was this morning that Mistress Margory left, wasn't it? I thought we could go for a walk as soon as she'd left."

"Mistress left me so much to do while she's away that I don't think I shall be able to take a walk for six months, never mind three!"

"Oh yes you will, my dear, sweet Hannah." Arthur lowered his voice. "We shall take a walk in the woods this very evening. Unlike last year, this year has been so dry that it will be a perfect time for walking in the woods. I can't wait to take your hand."

"Oh yes, Arthur, but no-one must see. The maids at The Manor chatter so much that word is sure to reach Mistress when she returns. The only person I shall tell will be Lucy who's becoming a very good friend of mine."

"Funny how she looks so much like you, you could be sisters. Sometimes I think I may get the two of you mixed up, but then, when I get closer to you, I can see how very much prettier you are."

Arthur moved closer.

"Oh Arthur, you do say such lovely things. I've never thought of myself as being pretty but – don't stand so very near to me as someone might see. I'm very worried that

Mistress wouldn't like me talking to you at all and she certainly wouldn't want me to stand as close to you as this."

"Whyever not, Hannah?" Arthur moved even closer. "This isn't close. I'll show you how close we could be when we walk out this evening."

Hannah's face became suffused like a peach as she glanced down. She had never stood as near to a boy as this. Arthur had now stood this close about three times and she was beginning to like it. She could feel his breath on her face and she liked the way he gently pushed back a little of her hair. But what, she wondered, if someone saw?

Chapter 29

"Lucy. Arthur has just asked me to walk with him. If Lady Francis or anyone needs me, would you come to get me right away? And please don't tell anyone where I am and with Arthur, will you? Mistress left me so much to do that, when she gets back, if she finds I went walking sometimes, I don't think she'll like it. I'm a bit frightened of Mistress Margory."

"Yes, I know what you mean. Don't you worry for a minute though, Hannah. We all know how hard you work and I don't know anybody who will chatter about you. They're too busy whispering about the Mistress! Oh here comes Arthur now. Enjoy yourself! He's very handsome. I wish I was walking out on the arm of a tall, good looking boy like Arthur. But I've seen how he looks at you, Hannah. He's got eyes for nobody else."

"Oh, do you think so, Lucy? He says such lovely things to me that I hardly trust myself to look into his eyes as it makes me go all swimmy. Here he comes. Don't forget, Lucy. Please let me know if Lady Francis or anybody else needs me. We shall be in the grounds, near the flower beds and ornaments so we shouldn't be difficult to find. Arthur mentioned going into the woods but I don't trust myself to go there now it's getting dark."

"I think that's a good idea, Hannah. I'll cover for you, don't you worry. Just have a lovely time."

"Here you are, Hannah. And was that Lucy I saw scurrying away? Here, take my arm and let's go into the woods."

"If you don't mind, Arthur, I would just like to walk around the beautiful grounds this evening. Is that all right?"

Arthur's face dropped a little. Hannah glanced at him and her heart echoed the dip. He looked so disappointed.

"Another time, Arthur. I would like to walk in the woods with you another time. Just not today. There are seats in the gardens where we can sit and talk. I would so like to get to know you better. Please don't be disappointed."

And so the three months began. To Arthur it seemed like three hours, he loved walking and talking with Hannah so much. Until one evening, Hannah met him and appeared to be quite excited.

Chapter 30

"What is it, Hannah? What's happened?"

"Well, I'm a bit surprised really." Hannah's eyes seemed to have grown even bigger.

"What, what? Tell me."

"I've been doing a lot of work for Lady Francis today, sorting out her clothes, making sure they're all perfect, then…"

"I'm sorry, Hannah, but I'm just not interested in Lady Francis's clothes. Why are you so excited?"

"I'd just finished putting everything away in her wardrobe when she asked me what I was going to do next. Right away, I asked her whether she had other tasks for me to do because I was happy to do them. She said I'd been a great help to her today and didn't need me for the rest of the day. She said she'd noticed that I go for walks with you and that, provided I did all the work she needed me to do, she thought it was a very nice idea for me to walk with you. In fact, I think I heard her say, sort of under her breath, that she wished her daughter was walking out with someone. But she said it so softly I couldn't be sure. Anyway, I was really surprised that she was telling me she was happy for me to walk with you that it didn't matter. She then patted me on the back, told me that I'd done very well today and was free to join you. I noticed that she looked at me strangely when she said that, and I didn't know why. But anyway, I just thanked her and came out here to join you. What do you think about that?"

Arthur couldn't believe his ears. For the Lady of the Manor to actually suggest that he and Hannah should walk out together was more than he could have dreamed for. How wonderful! That would mean Hannah needn't worry about Lady Francis needing her and, perhaps, disapproving if she couldn't be found.

Hannah broke into his thoughts.

"That doesn't mean that I can walk with you often, Arthur. Much as I would like to. It just means that Lady Francis is perfectly happy for me to do that – and has said so – when I have finished my work at The Manor.

"Of course, Hannah. I realise that, but it does make things so much easier, doesn't it, knowing that we needn't worry in case we're seen and that Lucy needn't come rushing to get us if we're out walking and Lady Francis needs you."

Reaching the seat in the grounds where they usually met, Hannah sat down, with Arthur sitting closely by her side.

"I'm beginning to think of this seat as ours, Arthur," Hannah said shyly, giving him a sidelong glance. "I hadn't realised how worried I was in case anyone saw us and told Lady Francis. I do feel much more relaxed now."

With that, she turned and took his hand.

"I would like to take that walk you spoke of into the woods tomorrow, Arthur."

Chapter 31

Arthur had never felt so tender, loving or giving. As he took Hannah's hand, he guided her into the woodland where he felt that the birds were singing especially for them. Hannah was, to him, as fragile as the porcelain dolls he had seen at the manor. She was to be treated with the utmost respect and gentleness, a thing of delicacy and wonderment. He felt surges of emotions unlike any others he had ever felt. He wanted to nurture her, to take care of her and never, ever to let her go. He couldn't bear to tear his eyes away from her exquisite little face which looked at him with such longing he thought he would explode. He wanted to protect her and to let the whole world know that she was his and his alone.

Arthur couldn't believe that here she was, lying next to him; he hardly dared to touch her lest she broke. Gradually, he failed to hear the bird song as all became quiet around the two of them; they were so close that even a leaf couldn't separate them. He looked at his hands. His fingers had become feathers. Were they clean? He didn't want to touch her perfect skin unless his body was worthy. He removed his cap and ran his fingers through his dark curls.

"Oh Arthur, you are so very handsome. What lovely hair you have," Hannah whispered, as though her words might break the glass of silence. Gently, she ran her index finger down the length of his face, ending by running all of them through his hair very slowly. The whole world seemed to have stopped turning so that the birds and trees could experience the fragility of their love. Arthur's body was melting like butter. He never wanted this to end. So slowly that neither of them were aware of the other's movements, they held each other close. Even their breathing seemed to emanate from one body. Gradually, they removed each other's clothing gently until only the air covered them.

Beginning with her hair, Arthur explored every single part of Hannah's body. Then, after what seemed like hours, he ran his fingers, one by one, from her toes to her face until neither could endure their two bodies being apart any longer. Arthur became one with Hannah so very tenderly that she didn't even realise his body was inside hers, only that that was where she wanted it to be so very much. Now they were one.

Chapter 32

"Get out of bed you lazy, stupid woman."

Arthur threw back the fine linen sheets and leaned in close to Margory's face. Her eyes popped open and she screamed so loudly that several servants came rushing into her bedchamber, the door crashing against the wall.

"Get out. All of you. This is my wife and I shall deal with her exactly as I wish. Do you hear? Get out! And never try to come to the aid of your Mistress again or you'll be sorry."

Arthur had always intended to treat servants politely, but this was different. Also, since becoming a member of the gentry, he didn't find it so easy to know how to treat servants. Clearly, an unusual friendship had grown between Margory and the servants. That changed things. They needed to know who was in charge and he would be that instrument of change. How odd that their servants had become friends of the gentry. No, that had to stop.

Margory raised herself on her elbows. She was speaking so quietly that the servants, about to turn away, turned and moved back a little, trying to hear what she was saying.

"Please obey Master Arthur. He is, of course, my husband and must be obeyed. At all times. I do not want to lose any of you, my faithful servants, who have helped me through so very many difficult times that I've lost count. Always remember that I think you are good people and that I wish to keep you in my employ as long as possible. In order for that to happen, it is necessary for you to do as my husband wishes. Do you understand?"

"But…" Yes, thought Arthur, this was definitely the time for change.

"No 'buts'. Do as she says. Get out of your mistress's bed chamber and leave us be. She has now not arisen for several days and I intend to ensure that she gets up and returns to her wifely duties. While you are here, I intend, too, for the servant called Lucy and my two children, Barbara and Joyce, to eat with my wife and me. I do not wish to see anyone else eating at the head of the table. I'm sure you are used to taking your meals at the servants' table end, but that will now cease. Is that clear? You will all take your meals in the kitchens. Not only that, you will partake of the leftovers from the meals of my wife, Lucy, our two children and myself. Although this is a manor house, it clearly does not have sufficient money to feed the large number of staff my wife has kept in her service. Also, although I wish servants no ill, you have become closer to my wife than is usual and that must change."

"Arthur, they are not only servants they are…"

"Are you interrupting me yet again, wife?"

With that he strode to the bedside and slapped her face. Hard.

The servants gasped. Margory's face immediately bore all the finger marks of Arthur's strike. She didn't move.

"Please do as my husband bids and leave us."

"Good. Finally, you are learning about the submission of wives. Just a few more words from you, a few more hard slaps and you may continue to learn. But you are such a stupid woman that I fear it will take many more slaps to teach you a lesson. And maybe I need to learn what other punishments will bring you in line with my commands. Just like horses, women need to be controlled. This is just a beginning, my dear, darling wife."

Chapter 33

The sound of horses had brought Arthur and Hannah to their feet with a leap.

"Oh no, I lost track of time. I forgot that Mistress Margory is back today from Gloucestershire. If she finds out you and I have been in the woods so many times, Arthur, she won't like it. I know she won't like it at all. She'll probably send me away. It's three months since she left..."

"Yes, Hannah, and they've been three wonderful months, haven't they? Why are you shaking? As Lady Francis has been perfectly happy for us to walk out together, why are you so worried?"

"I don't know. I just have this very strong feeling that Mistress Margory won't like it."

Hannah brushed down her dress and tripped. Arthur caught her before she fell, and found himself looking into her wide, worried eyes.

"You're looking pale, Hannah. Are you all right?"

"Yes, I think so, but I haven't felt well for the last few weeks. Also, something has been missing, but I can't talk to you about that, as you're a man."

Although Arthur couldn't be sure, he thought he knew what Hannah meant. Perhaps their coming together had produced a child. He would have to think about that. He couldn't ask his mother any questions because she would immediately be suspicious as to why he was asking. No. She would know why he was asking.

"Arthur. Did you hear me? You seemed to go off into another world then. Have I got all the leaves and twigs off my skirt? I'm going into the kitchens to see if I can help cook. I've got to seem to be doing one of my usual tasks before Mistress Margory calls for me. Goodbye for now, Arthur. Now that Mistress Margory is back, I don't know when we shall be able to walk out. I still feel frightened of her."

Arthur didn't understand how anyone could be frightened of another human being. He had never been frightened of anyone. He certainly wasn't frightened of any woman he had met. In spite of his feelings for Hannah, he still thought that women were to be controlled, like horses.

Chapter 34

Margory didn't move. Her body remained curled like a cat. But there was no purring.

"What is the matter, my dear? Now that we're alone, you can tell me why you aren't getting out of bed. I would so love to get inside you again as I did a few nights ago. Just think. If you don't agree again, I shall have to tell the servants to make up another bedchamber. I may even tell Lucy that she has to join me. Or maybe that other pretty maid I spoke to the day I arrived. What do you have to say to that, dear wife?"

"Perhaps you enjoyed being humiliated in front of the servants, did you? Perhaps you liked being slapped. Oh, I can see a bruise beginning to appear on your cheek already. What a shame. Next time, I shall hit you where it can't be seen by anyone. Of course, I shall take off your clothes and look at it when I want to. In fact, I may tear off your clothes. Would you like that, my dear? Of course, I would wait until you had changed into your night chemise so that it wouldn't take long for me to see your naked body but... Oh, don't cry, my darling. Sometimes I wouldn't tell the servants why you are screaming. But, if I'm not happy with your behaviour, I shall ask them all to come into this very bedchamber and I shall lock the door so that they can't escape. And you wouldn't be able to either. What a shame."

Margory's eyes suddenly snapped open.

"What did I ever do to you that you wish to hurt me so very much?"

"Well, where shall I begin? I found horses much more appealing than you. I'm not sure why, really, because your face isn't unlike that of a horse. Then there was the time when you whistled for me at one of your parties. You whistled! I think that will require extra punishment. Would you like something to eat, dear wife?"

Mumbling met his question.

"What? Speak more loudly otherwise I shall have to bite that mouth that eats."

"No, I'm not hungry at all."

"Good. In that case, I shall instruct Cook not to give you any meals until I say so. What do you think?" With that, he moved closer.

"I don't feel hungry at all. In fact I feel a little sick."

She then vomited all over Arthur.

"Ugggh! Oh, what a bad lady you are. In fact, ladies don't do that. As a punishment I won't be telling the servants to clear up your mess. You must lie in it for as long as I wish. Oh dear, what a nasty smell! I shall have to search out Lucy and our children to walk in the sweet-smelling gardens. I shall be locking the door so that you won't be seen in such a dreadful state. But first, I shall go and change my clothes."

"I'd like to bathe."

"What a pity. You see, you must be taught a lesson. Who is the lord and master here?"

Silence.

"I asked you a question, wife. Oh, I've just had a wonderful idea. Your friend who isn't your lover – what is his name? Hugh? – will, I have no doubt, come searching for you to save you from your wicked husband. What I shall do is tell Goodwife Sykes to show him to this very bedchamber. Now if he's a gentleman, he will refuse. But if he's curious, he may just want to rush to your aid. Yes, in fact, I may just send him a note in your name, asking him to meet you here, in this very room. What a good idea! The more I think on't, the more I warm to it. He will receive your note, come rushing to help you and will be shown to this foul-smelling bedchamber where you lie. I'll get your maid to make sure the bruise on your face doesn't show. You can sit up in bed and receive him with a beautiful smile. Wouldn't you like that, dear Margory?"

Margory was sobbing so loudly she thought the entire manor would hear her.

"What is it, dear one? I thought you would like to see your beloved Hugh. I may even join you both to show what a very good, considerate, thoughtful and solicitous husband I am. Wouldn't you like that? Or would you prefer not to see him at all? No, I think that a loving note from you, asking him to come to you as quickly as he can because you're in danger, will encourage him to choose his fastest horse so that he can be by your side to protect you. Wouldn't you like that? I know you would. So that is what I shall do this very day. Come, wife, am I not being a very considerate and understanding husband in sending for the man you care for to help you in your hour of need? Now, I really must leave this horrible smell and change my attire. Mmm. What wonderful smells there are from Cook's biscuits and sweetmeats. I am quite reminded of when I first came to The Manor and served them to your guests. What a long time ago that was, and how things have changed. But perhaps not everything has changed. You were left standing on your own most of the time, weren't you, at your own party. And why was that, Margory? Why, because your face never was pretty and your fondness of sweetmeats was so strong that you were fat. Yes, Margory, fat. And now you're alone once more."

"I loved you."

"What was that? I can't hear what you're saying when you curl up like that and mumble." He took her face in his hand and pressed his thumb into her bruise, forcing her to look at him.

"What did you say?"

"I loved you."

"Nonsense. No-one else would have you and you thought you could command me – like a dog – to do your bidding. Gradually, you discovered that you could not. I didn't like being treated like a dog. No-one should be treated like a dog. Get out of bed this minute, Margory, and bark like a dog."

"What?"

"You heard me. Instead of lying there, day in, day out, like the lazy person you are. Get out of bed, get down on all fours and bark like a dog. While you're doing that, I shall write this message to your gentleman friend, Hugh."

"Please don't, Arthur. I'll do anything you want, but Hugh is a good man. Please."

"You'll do anything I want, will you. Good. I shall remember that and remind you when the time is right. But, as I said. Now, I shall write a note from you to Hugh."

Chapter 35

"Is that the door already? Oh, how very quickly your loved one has come to your aid, Margory. And there goes Goodwife Sykes to welcome him – as I'm sure she has welcomed him many times, my dear, in my absence. Isn't that so? I must unlock your chamber door so that nothing and nobody stands between you and he."

A light knock and Arthur opened the door almost as wide as Hugh's eyes on seeing him.

"No, don't you worry, Goodwife Sykes. Return to your duties. I shall deal with this."

"And why are you here yet again, sir, when you will recall my distinctly telling you not to come to my home ever again? Did I invite you? Stop your burbling, wife. Do you want this gentleman to hear your foolishness?"

Hugh strode to the bed, his face showing utter dismay at seeing his normally beautifully dressed friend, not only wearing unclean night attire but having spent, clearly, little time out of the bed for quite some time. He stepped back as the malodorous aroma hit his nostrils. As though on cue, Margory vomited once more, this time covering Hugh in the vile smelling liquid.

Arthur laughed.

"You are very welcome to stay and talk to my dear wife, but she doesn't really seem to be feeling very hospitable at the moment, don't you agree?"

Hugh didn't move, but stood with the pale liquid running down his clothes. Margory could bear this game of Arthur's no longer.

"Please, oh please, Hugh, do leave."

"But you asked me to come here. Are you ill? What is going on, Margory? Shall I call your surgeon?"

As though in slow motion, Margory slipped to the floor, groaning and lay there, sobbing softly.

Hugh knelt down and took her in his arms,

"My dear Margory. Whatever is the matter? Can you tell me? You must be ill. I shall leave this moment and get help for you."

"She doesn't need your help and neither do I. Frankly, I don't know why you're here and suggest that you leave. To be honest, my wife has not been herself since my return and I fear she is not only ill physically but mentally, too. All she does is lie in bed, day in, day out, not speaking, not eating, and crying all the while. That she is unhappy for some reason seems to be very clear. But I'm sure she will recover. In the meantime, as I said, we do not need your help and your presence is beginning to annoy me. As this is the second time you have appeared unwanted, should it happen again, I shall set the dogs on you."

"Margory, do you wish me to go?"

The look that Margory gave him was so utterly despairing that it left Hugh completely puzzled.

"Yes, Hugh. You should go."

"So there you are. 'Tis not only I who wishes you gone, but my wife requests it. I won't ask Goodwife Sykes to show you out as you clearly know your way around my house. And this time, stay away or I won't be responsible for my actions."

Margory thought her heart would break as she heard Hugh's horse galloping away.

"So now, dearest, it's just you and I. And isn't that the way it should be with husbands and wives?

Margory vomited again.

Chapter 36

Much to Arthur's surprise, Margory took to her bed again and wasn't seen for some time, despite his threats. Until, one day, there was a hammering on the great door and, when the butler, James, opened it, a man, announcing himself as Lord Winchester's physician, demanded to be shown to the lady of the house. James deemed it appropriate to show the gentleman – for clearly he was a gentleman – to the library in the first instance. As they got there, Arthur came bounding down the staircase, to be met by Goodwife Sykes.

"Who is it now wanting to see my wife? I do declare she seems to have many visitors, none of whom are invited."

"The gentleman's name is Dr Simmons. He is Lord Winchester's physician."

"Oh yes, clearly this is the doing of my wife's gentleman friend, Hugh Taylor, who has told him to call. How very impertinent!" Pushing open the library door, Arthur demanded,

"And why, pray, do we need Lord Winchester's physician when we have a perfectly capable doctor of our own?"

"Good day, sir. My name is …"

"I've been told your name."

"May I know who you are?"

"I am the Lord of the Manor, Arthur Wright, and I have a right to be here whereas I would like to know why I find you in my library, uninvited."

"I regret that you are receiving me in such a manner, sir. Lord Winchester and his estate manager…"

"Ah yes, of course. His estate manager. I assume you are referring to Mr Hugh Taylor. He also came uninvited, asking to see my wife. As she has been lying lazily abed for quite some time, he also entered her bedchamber – perhaps not for the first time and…"

"Please take me to your wife as it is inappropriate for me to enter into any further conversation with you about matters that are of no concern to me. I assume your wife is still unwell?"

"I believe so as she doesn't move herself from her bed and hasn't done so for several weeks. Oh, all right. There's no harm in your seeing her with me."

"Your presence, sir, will be inappropriate. Would someone ask the housekeeper to be in attendance. She seemed to be a capable woman of sufficient years to help me, if that is needed."

"I wish to be there."

"And I insist, sir, that it is not appropriate for a gentleman to be present when I am examining your wife."

Pleased at being called a gentleman, Arthur succumbed and asked Lucy, who had just appeared with the two children, to summon Goodwife Sykes.

"What delightful children. I assume they are yours and your wife's?"

"Erm," Arthur wriggled uncomfortably, "Here is Goodwife Sykes who will accompany you to my wife's bedchamber. Goodwife Sykes, the doctor has asked that you remain with him while he is examining my wife. When you have done that, please show him out."

"I shall leave once I have discussed with you any difficulties your wife may have."

"I care not what they are. She is clearly very lazy. All I want is for her to resume her duties as soon as possible, organising the servants' work and menus with cook."

"I see. In that case, I shall send you a copy of my written report."

"That won't be necessary. I think my wife is simply avoiding me so I am not expecting a medical diagnosis to be relevant."

"As you wish. However, this is highly irregular…"

"I would remind you, sir, that I, as the head of the household, did not request your presence. Additionally, if you persist in remaining, I shall have you thrown out – just as I told Lord Winchester's estate manager very recently." Softly, Goodwife Sykes urged the doctor to accompany her.

Chapter 37

"I care not what your master wished. It is important that I speak to him now that I have examined his wife. I am already late for another appointment, so please make haste – Goodwife Sykes, isn't it? – and tell your master that I wish to speak to him as a matter of urgency."

Goodwife Sykes went in search of Arthur as quickly as she could. Arthur banged the library door in annoyance.

"What is it? I understood you to say that you would not waste my time further and that you would send a written report. I can read, of course – Arthur drew himself up proudly – so that is all I expect of you."

"You, sir, are wasting *my* time and I must leave now for another appointment. Your wife is expecting a child and…"

"What?" Arthur sat down heavily. "Are you sure?"

"I've had quite enough of your rudeness, sir. I repeat. Your wife is with child which, as far as I can tell, is due in about 28 weeks' time. Additionally, she is clearly distressed and I suggest that she is left to rest for as long as she feels that to be necessary. I suggest, too, that, as she is having such a very difficult time, that I preside over the birth. After that, I can recommend an excellent midwife. Unless, of course, that is beyond your financial means."

"Rest! Why? Lucy continued her duties…And, of course, whatever you charge will be perfectly acceptable," Arthur added hastily.

"Who is Lucy and what does she have to do with your wife's condition? I haven't got time to stand here discussing other births. Good day, sir."

Chapter 38

How long Arthur remained in the library, he did not know. What he did know was that he had been the only person to go near his wife for the last few weeks. He knew that definitely, as he had locked the bedchamber door each and every time he had left. No, this had to be the result of his having taken her against her will. Well well well. This changed everything. He now had a legitimate heir to The Manor. That should keep his wife's admirer, Hugh, away. What an interesting turn of events. He didn't think she had it in her. On the other hand, within the first year of their marriage she had miscarried. Yes, he had almost forgotten that.

Bounding up the stairway, Arthur unlocked Margory's bedchamber door and took a seat near his wife. He peered at her. Her eyes were closed but he didn't think she was sleeping.

"Well, wife. What news! We are to have a child. I have an heir. You must be overjoyed."

At that, Margory's eyes opened very slowly and glared at him with such ferocity he drew back in alarm.

"Overjoyed? I would rather be dead than bear a child of yours. Babes should be born of love. There was no love whatsoever involved in your forcing yourself upon me. Give birth to your child? Perhaps I shall fall, as I did before, and it will die. I do not wish to bear this child. And I do not wish it because it is yours. Do you understand? If it dies, I shall be glad and shall hope to die also. I loathe and detest you. Any child I bear of yours will be cursed, for it will be born of hatred. Do you understand? This child will be born of pure hatred. That's because you are evil, Arthur Wright."

Arthur drew back. For the first time in his life, he felt fear. Never had he witnessed such repugnance. Margory's face was screwed up and knotted in a way he had never seen before. Her words were not spoken but spat from her mouth that seemed to have shrunk to the size of a very small 'o'. He backed away even further in horror. This was not the wife who had persuaded him into marriage, who had done his bidding and longed for their coupling. The woman before him was an entirely different person and one he didn't recognise at all. Heaven help the child born of this creature. But born the babe would be, even if he had to deliver it himself. He shook himself, like a dog shaking off the rain. Of course he wouldn't be in charge of the delivery. He would send for the family physician that very day as well as a midwife. Whatever his wife said, this child would be his heir. Nothing and no-one would come between him and his scion. Neither the physician nor anyone else would ever know how this babe had been conceived. What did it matter anyway?

Chapter 39

For the first 20 weeks Margory's vomiting dominated her days. As a midwife, she knew that the sickness usually only came in the mornings. But instead, she was suffering the whole day – sometimes as often as 40 times a day. There was nothing she could do about it other than succumb. If only her dear mother were still here. She would know what to do. But in all the pregnancies with which her mother had helped and Margory had dealt with, she had never seen sickness like this. She couldn't eat and couldn't even keep down the water that her personal maid, Ruth, was boiling for her. She grew used to Arthur's coming and going, complaining about her never arising, stamping off and telling her that Lucy hadn't been such a trouble when she was with child. All women were sick when expecting a child, he kept telling her. What a nuisance she was.

Margory's days came and went in a haze of such utter unpleasantness that she genuinely wished the Lord would intervene and take her from this world. The only person she saw was Lord Winchester's physician who visited and left like a ghost. On one of these visits, Margory asked why she was experiencing such severe sickness, at which he shook his head and said he had never encountered it before. All he did was to assure her that when he was summoned to deliver the child she could be sure he would arrive quickly and would do all in his power to ease the delivery so that she suffered as little as possible. In the meantime, he told Goodwife Sykes to give her mistress as much boiled water as possible, as often as possible. On one occasion, Margory did think she saw Hugh standing by her bedside, but the sight of his dear face made her feel even worse and even he seemed puzzled.

The day of delivery dawned and, at noon exactly, on Tuesday, 1st June 1565, with Margory's maids encircling the bed, a howling and screeching was heard, when a baby was not so much born as ejected from Margory's body like a cannon. A gasp went around the bedchamber as the maids turned to the physician in amazement. Indeed, his face was a puzzle of perplexity. Never before had he seen anything that looked like this child.

Chapter 40

"Is my baby born? Is it a boy or a girl?"

Truth to tell, neither the doctor nor servants were very sure to start with. A black, oily substance seemed to cover most of the little body, leaving only the tiny nose and very large mouth free to breathe and screech. Indeed, this blob of black flesh seemed to be not so much a baby as the personification of a howling animal.

Recovering quickly, the physician took control once more, telling one of the maids to bring more water, towels and linen bands to wrap the child in. When she hurried off, muttering that she didn't want to go anywhere near the "creature", she was followed by the others. Only Goodwife Sykes remained. She hadn't felt fear for many years and didn't intend to be frightened by a tiny baby now. Nevertheless, she didn't feel inclined to go near either, simply doing as the doctor asked. She then moved to the head of the bed and cooled Margory's wet face, whispering "All is well. You have a lusty baby."

At that, Margory opened her eyes slightly and, on seeing her faithful servant, she smiled, "Thank you Goodwife Sykes. What a wonderful friend you are. I'd like to hold my baby now. As you know, this will be the very first time I have held a babe of my own, although I have, of course, held many others belonging to other mothers. This is a very special moment for me."

As Goodwife Sykes returned to the newborn, the physician had just finished cleaning it. While still rather strange-looking, the child was clearly male and gazed at her with large, dark eyes. When the physician handed him to her, Goodwife Sykes almost dropped him as he let out yet another alarmingly loud howl. She was amazed that such a small being could create such an ear-splitting sound. Quickly taking him to Margory, she placed him gently into her arms, at which the child stopped, as though his screaming had been turned off like a tap. He then turned, looked at Margory and smiled – the sweetest smile Goodwife Sykes had ever seen a baby only 10 minutes old give anyone. This was no ordinary child, she thought, while making Margory comfortable.

"Did you see that, Goodwife Sykes? He is smiling at me already. I have never seen that happen so quickly before. My baby is certainly very special, don't you think?" Goodwife Sykes nodded. This baby was, indeed, unusual.

Suddenly the door of the bedchamber banged open and in strode Arthur.

"Well, well. I see I have a son and heir who is very healthy. Isn't that correct, sir?"

The doctor had just finished packing his bag and, turning to Arthur, said, "Congratulations on a healthy baby boy. Already he appears advanced and, I'm sure, will prove to be a worthy son. This is no ordinary child. I shall now take my leave and send my invoice in due course."

"Of course he's no ordinary child! He is my child. And my first son. He will have everything he wants, always. He will be raised in the lap of luxury and no-one will stand in his way – ever!"

If the doctor raised his eyebrows at this, no-one noticed. He had experienced many proud fathers before. This one was no exception, if a little more arrogant than most. Neither, he noticed, had this man enquired after his wife's health.

Chapter 41

Margory held her baby so close she thought he would break. She felt an overwhelming sense of protectiveness and love such as she had never ever felt before in her entire 25 years. Gone were the thoughts of how he had been conceived. He was here and he was hers. She couldn't quite believe it.

"Well, wife. I have an heir."

Arthur's commanding voice shattered like glass the total tenderness Margory felt as she gazed into her baby's face. *Her* baby. At last. All these years she had longed for and waited for a child of her own and here he was, nestling into her bosom as though it had been made just for him. And it had. Even Arthur's presence couldn't change her depth of feeling. Difficult as it was to drag away her eyes from her precious bundle, she looked at Arthur as though she had never seen him before. This was not so much her husband standing by her side, but the father of her child. She must never forget that. She must do exactly as Arthur commanded, provided, of course, her baby came to no harm. That she would not tolerate. No, this was a new day created by her new son. Generously, she invited Arthur,

"Would you like to hold your son, Arthur?"

"Absolutely not! He's my heir, not my toy. I insist that you, yourself, bathe and dress him, keep him clean at all times, teach him as you taught me and never, ever let him out of your sight. Love is a feeling I have experienced once in my life and do not intend to risk going down that path again, only to have it torn from me, as happened before. It is enough to have loved once and is not a weakness I intend to endure a second time. No, you can shower our son with all your love as he certainly won't be receiving my love in this life. You are welcome to him. And now I shall go to the inn and let everyone know that, not only am I Lord of the

Manor, but I have a male heir. I shall tell all I see so that gossip, being the creature it is, will fly through the village until it reaches the ears of your friend, Hugh. I would like to be there when he hears that his dear friend, Margory, has had a son by her husband."

Only then was Margory's overwhelming love burned a little around the edges. Hugh. How could she have forgotten him? But forget him she must. The only person in her life now was this beautiful boy, lying in her arms and still gazing at her as though he could never tear away his eyes. Once more, her whole body felt awash with tenderness, like a tide that never went out, enveloping her in such a way that she could hardly breathe. If she could have wrapped him in a blanket and held him for the rest of his life, she would have done that. Born of an evil act he may have been, but this little angelic face looking up at her bore only the signs of total innocence. Or so she thought.

Chapter 42

The first time Arthur hit baby Henry, Margory almost killed him. The look of utter astonishment on the tiny face preceded a wailing that must have been heard throughout the county. He had received only gentle affection in his first five weeks, combined with soft words, kisses, cuddles and feathery fingers stroking his face. This was an entirely different feeling for him.

Margory immediately lifted Henry out of his cradle, pressing him into her shoulder which quickly became saturated with his tears. Holding him slightly away from her, she saw that a red mark was already turning purple on his sweet cheek. She was reminded of her own, very first bruised cheek inflicted by Arthur. But she was a grown woman. This was a small, vulnerable baby.

"Why did you do that? You're a grown man and he's a tiny child."

"Do my ears deceive me? Is my wife questioning my actions? This is not only your child, but mine, too, and I shall do to him whatever I wish, whenever I wish. Is that understood?"

"Do whatever you like to me, Arthur Wright, but never, ever touch Henry again in such a way. If you do, I won't be responsible for my actions. What did he do to you to encourage such a violent act?"

"He just lies there doing nothing. He sleeps. He smells. And the only person he smiles at is you. He needs to learn – as does every single person in this household – that I am in charge. Whatever I say, goes. When I don't wish something to happen, it will not happen. Do you understand?"

Silence.

"I said. Do you understand?"

A knock on the great door followed by the butler's

footsteps halted the conversation.

"Are you expecting a visitor, wife?"

"No. I don't yet feel well enough to receive visitors."

Goodwife Sykes's knock on the withdrawing room door elicited a "Come" from Margory.

"Mistress. Oh, I do beg your pardon, Master Arthur, I didn't see you standing there. It's the midwife come to check on baby Henry."

"Did you summon her, Margory, because I certainly did not."

"I seem to vaguely recall the doctor saying right after the birth that he would ask his midwife to check that all was going well with the baby."

"Well, I shall stay to hear what she has to say. Enough visitors have entered my manor without my invitation or knowledge and I wish it to stop. Now. Show her in here, Goodwife Sykes, and be quick about it."

"We shall have to get rid of that woman. She's getting old and very slow."

"She has been…"

"You are not contradicting me yet again, Margory, are you? If I say that Goodwife Sykes has to leave, leave she will. Neither do I wish midwives to visit."

A soft knock and the midwife was announced.

Arthur's countenance immediately changed when the young, pretty woman entered the room, giving him a blazing smile. At the same time, Margory was returned to her teenage years when she felt plain and fat. Arthur seemed to have turned into a fawning deer.

"Do come in, my dear, and take a seat. Goodwife Sykes. Refreshments for this delightful lady and I – and, oh yes, for Mistress Margory, too. And quickly. Now, I am so very sorry but my silly wife didn't say that we would be having such a gracious visitor this afternoon. Have you come to see our beautiful baby?"

"Thank you for your hospitality, sir, and what a fine home you have here, may I say. Yes, the doctor asked me to make sure that your baby is growing as he should."

"I'm sure that he will under your care. As this is our first child, my wife really knows very little about nurturing."

Sitting straighter, Margory said,

"I was, of course, a midwife for many years and did not preside over deaths when I was in charge of delivery from beginning to end. I inherited my skills from my mother and became licensed."

"Yes, yes, Margory. This lovely young lady isn't interested in your history, are you, my dear? While we are waiting for tea to be served, do take a look at our beautiful child. You will find nothing wrong, I'm sure."

"How did he come by this nasty bruise on his cheek?"

"Margory, that was when you dropped him this morning, wasn't it? Tell this midwife, my dear. Don't be ashamed of your clumsiness."

"I am a little clumsy, but I don't recall dropping the dear child."

"I'm sorry, not only is my wife clumsy but she seems to be losing her memory, too. Otherwise she's a very good mother. After all, no-one is perfect. Ah, here's our tea. Took you long enough, Goodwife Sykes. Think we must start looking for your replacement."

Margory shifted uneasily and patted her skirt, her mouth tightening.

Putting his little face up to hers, Henry smiled, before changing to a look of surprise as he saw a tear leave his mother's eye. He prodded it with a little, fat finger and smiled again, willing his mother to smile back. She couldn't resist this little man who meant the world to her.

"Well, he seems to have recovered from his fall now, and

that bruise will disappear before you know it. I must be on my way. I'll come again in six weeks' time to make sure that Henry is progressing as he should. That's if that is suitable to you, sir? But he seems to be perfectly healthy, other than the fall he had. You will need to be careful, Mistress Margory. If he falls again, the result could be worse."

"Er…"

"Yes, that's what I've told her. If she isn't more careful, I shall have to put him in the care of someone else in the household who will take better care of him. I'm going to the inn now. Shall I walk with you to wherever you're going next, dear lady? Good. You can't be too careful on these roads – lovely lady like you should be accompanied by someone who can protect her. Why, only the other day I was reminding my wife of the time her parents, she and I rode into London and were set upon by a group of thieves. You can rest assured that I despatched the leader quickly. Didn't I dear?"

"You did, Arthur."

"How very brave of you, sir."

Arthur drew himself up proudly.

Margory was beginning to realise that she would need to keep an eye on her errant husband. Undermining her confidence was one thing. Allowing outsiders to think that she was responsible for Henry's bruises was entirely different. And now Arthur was beginning to imply that she was losing her mind. Where would these comments end? Could she risk seeking out Hugh? Would he want to speak to her now? He probably thought – like everyone else – that she and Arthur were man and wife in every sense of the word, particularly since the birth of Henry. What was she to do? For the moment, however, she was pleased to see him leaving, and hoped that the young woman could take care of herself.

Chapter 43

"Oh, here we are at the inn. Are you sure I can't tempt you to have just one small drink, my dear? That's good. I knew you'd change your mind. As you're going to be looking after my sweet child, I think I should start getting to know you. Are you licensed? No? Well, I'm sure that a good word from me will walk you in that direction. Also, our child has not yet been baptised."…As the midwife looked at him in horror…"Yes, I know. My wife just keeps forgetting to arrange it. I do despair that she is losing her mind. Now, I didn't catch your name. Beth. What a beautiful name. Just like its owner."

As Arthur and the midwife walked into the overflowing pub, they were immediately surrounded by Arthur's friends.

"How goes it in the fields, lads? Oh yes, I now have an heir – this is his pretty midwife." Digging in the ribs accompanied this statement.

"Now, lads, that's no way to treat a Lord of the Manor. Show some respect. Beer all round, innkeeper and a large white wine for the lady. And serve them in silver, not pewter. No my dear, don't go yet, I insist. Oh well, if you must. When will you be visiting again? Six weeks? No, I suggest you return in two weeks in case my wife injures our child again. Next time, we shall take my carriage to the inn so that we can get to know each other better. Remember what I told you about your becoming licensed. Goodbye then. Until next time."

"Congratulations, Arthur, on your son and heir."

With a big grin on his face and turning quickly to acknowledge yet another such compliment, Arthur's face fell as he saw that it was Hugh who had spoken the words.

Chapter 44

Now that Henry was becoming more active, he became restless quicker, so Margory decided to take him into Greenwillows. Just as she was passing the church, she ran into an old friend who was looking so well she hardly recognised her.

"Is that you, Marion? And this fine, little man can't be Jacob?"

The two women embraced and stood back to look for similarities and changes in the way they had both looked two years before – as women do.

"My dear Margory, how wonderful to see you after all this time. I was only thinking about you the other day and wondering how we had lost touch. You look a little pale. Are you well? And is this your little one? How absolutely delighted you must be to have had a child of your own at last. I am so very pleased for you, Margory."

Knowing that her good friend would notice how she was avoiding some of these questions, Margory hastily said,

"Dear Marion. Why are you here in Greenwillows?"

"Lord Winchester has asked Abner to look at some horses in a very good stable here. He kindly loaned his carriage for us so that Jacob and I could come along, too, and I'm doing a little shopping while I'm here. It was all arranged quite quickly, otherwise I would have tried to contact you as we haven't met for such a long time. I've missed you, Margory. I do hope that all is going well."

"Marion. You're just the wise, discreet friend I need to confide in at the moment. Can I arrange to see you in Brockminster some time soon?"

"That will be lovely, Margory. What about next Tuesday? Come for a meal at mid-day."

"I shall look forward to that very much, Marion. So much has been happening that – and you won't believe this – dear Henry hasn't been baptised yet and I'm thinking that the following week will be a good time."

Margory knew that Marion's suggestion would be perfect as Arthur had said he had to do some business in the north-west connected with his previous home where he'd lived with Lucy and their two children. She hadn't asked what he would be doing because, frankly, she wasn't interested. All she cared about now was Henry and making sure that he was happy and safe. Marion was exactly the person she needed to talk to at the moment. After all, she was the one who, due to her wonderful friendship, had got out of her sick bed to give facts at her trial that had ensured she was not convicted of witchcraft. Margory's servants had become very good friends to her but Marion was a special friend. Yes, this meeting had come at exactly the right time.

"Thank you, Marion. I shall look forward to that very much."

Chapter 45

The following Tuesday dawned frosty, bright and clear and I just knew it was going to be a lovely day. I felt more cheerful than I had for quite some time and that, in turn, transmitted to dear little Henry. He had just started to realise that he could crawl around on his own and, every so often, he would look at me over his shoulder and give a big grin as if to say, "Look how clever I am!"

Arthur had not joined me in bed that night and, when breaking our fast, he said he was going North with Lucy and the children and didn't know when they would be back.

"You look particularly pleased with yourself this morning, Margory. Why is that?"

"I suppose because it's such a beautiful day."

"And what are you going to do with this beautiful day? You seem to spend a great deal of time with Henry but very little in organising the household. When I return I shall expect to see a change. Do you understand? I had considered taking Henry with us but I can't be bothered."

"He will only slow you down, Arthur. Being so small, he needs a lot of personal attention, attention that I'm able to give him."

"You certainly are agreeable today, Margory. Is there something I should know?"

"Not at all, Arthur. I shall start speaking to the servants the moment you have gone. You're quite right in saying that I have been giving a great deal of attention to Henry and, perhaps, the household hasn't been as well organised as it should be. I shall deal with that while you're away."

"I'm glad to hear it. When we return, I shall expect you to tell me what you have done, not leaving anything out. I'm still rather puzzled that you seem much more jovial than usual. Maybe I shall take to our bed on my return where, hopefully, your change in mood will make our coming together much more convivial than it has been of late."

I said nothing. If anything was going to shatter my happiness, it was the prospect of Arthur joining me in the bedchamber. Still, that wouldn't be for a little while. In the meantime, I was going to enjoy talking to my good friend, Marion.

Chapter 46

"Goodwife Sykes. Would you take care of Henry today, please? I have to speak to someone and he would become restless. My husband is away for a few days so when I return, you and I will sit down and start to put The Manor in order. I haven't felt like speaking to you or cook for some time and I thank you for continuing to keep the house and kitchens running smoothly while I have been indisposed. Also, I have arranged for Henry to be baptised next week. At last I am becoming organised again."

"Mistress. You know that you do not need to thank me or any of the other servants, for that matter. We know that you have been experiencing very trying times but we are delighted to see little Henry growing into a beautiful little boy. Of course, I shall be happy to take care of him in your absence, although I shall ask one of our younger servants to help me as my old bones don't move as quickly as they did and Henry is now beginning to move around very quickly indeed. While that is wonderful to see, he could get lost very fast in this large house! I shall distract him while you take your leave as he will certainly be upset to see you go."

"Yes, that's a good idea. He's just beginning to get his first teeth so, while he's usually a happy baby, he's a little ill-humoured at times, understandably."

"I shall take him to the nursery now with Eleanor so that he doesn't see you leave."

"Yes, would you ask one of the stable boys to bring my horse, please?"

"Of course. May I enquire where you are going, Mistress?"

"Better that you don't know, Goodwife Sykes, on this occasion. I shall return later today."

Chapter 47

Margory hadn't ridden for some time, but she quickly regained her expertise and love of feeling the wind in her long, dark hair as she flew over The Manor's acres. Just as she was leaving the estate, she saw the beautiful trees sway towards her, at the same time whispering "beware" in exactly the way they had on her wedding day. At the same time, she saw one of the stable hands – or perhaps he was one of the new servants her husband had employed recently – crouched behind the trees. Arthur was right. She had not been her usual, efficient self for quite some time. She would rectify that as soon as she returned. She had always known every one of the servants and, indeed, enjoyed getting to know them. It was something she had taken particular pride in doing since her parents' demise. Yes, she felt more decisive today. She had become totally entwined in baby Henry's day-to-day life since the moment he was born and had forgotten everything else. She thanked the Lord that she had finally remembered to arrange his baptism for the following week so that his sins would be forgiven. But how could her dear, dear Henry have any sins? Nevertheless, his baptism was vital and she was pleased that she had finally got around to arranging that. However, although it was important to Margory, Arthur didn't care whether Henry was baptised or not – indeed, it had slipped her mind to mention next week's date to him. She must do that as soon as he returned. Yes, she was looking forward to speaking to Marion today. Then she must ensure that her household was running efficiently on her return. She would even try to be a little more understanding to Arthur.

She had avoided her husband whenever she could and spent every waking moment with her son. Perhaps things were changing for the better. But, the black cloud that always hung over her head was the sight of Arthur's slapping Henry. Not only that, but Arthur's lie to the midwife. She was very concerned about his allegation to an outside person. As he was capable of that sort of lie when she was present, she couldn't imagine what he would say in her absence. It was these cruel events that Margory hastened to tell Marion about. Her sensible friend would know what she should do.

Chapter 48

Still a little way off from Lord Winchester's land on which Marion and Abner's cottage was nestled, Margory saw Abner in the distance, with another man on horseback. Again, it had been some time since she had seen Marion's husband. What a very pleasant day today would be. She waved at Abner and he gave a cheery wave in return, at which both he and the other rider galloped to greet her. It was only as they drew closer that Margory saw it was Hugh. Suddenly, her bright and beautiful day came crashing down around her. Those waves of sadness were joined by such delight at seeing his kind face again that Margory didn't know what to do. She reigned in her horse and waited, looking down at the ground as she could not bear the possibility of seeing Hugh's disappointed face. She also knew that she was not looking her best at the moment as the time preceding baby Henry's birth had been months of lying in bed feeling distraught and ill. Although that was now five months ago, she had neither seen nor done anything other than with Henry. Apart from the all-consuming love she felt for him, she tried to keep him away from Arthur in case he annoyed him enough to repeat the slap – or worse – that he had given him. It had become increasingly clear that, to Arthur, Henry was merely another step up the ladder of gentrification. While his own claim to be Lord of the Manor may not be very acceptable to Hertfordshire's gentry, they could not deny the fact that he now had an heir to the land. Henry was the key that opened more doors to further greatness. What went on behind Arthur's own manorial doors stayed behind those doors, aided and abetted by lies.

"Margory. My dear Margory. How are you?"

Instead of the black cloud that she thought was hanging over her head and bursting with rain when Hugh saw her, his omnipresent smile as he looked at her was the ray of sunshine that had been missing from her life for a very long time. How could such goodness be encased in one person alone, she wondered? Once again, Margory rocked between her natural delight at seeing Hugh and the knowledge that he could never be more than her friend. Indeed, she really didn't think that even friendship was a realistic possibility.

With all these contradictory bees buzzing through her head, she suddenly realised that Hugh had spoken to her and she hadn't replied.

"I'm very well, Hugh. How kind of you to ask."

In the way he always had, Hugh took Margory by the waist and helped her dismount, their faces almost touching as her feet touched the ground. Suddenly, Margory was taken back to one of her very first encounters with Hugh when he had visited her land and helped her down from her horse in exactly the same way. The identical thought had run through her head on that occasion as was sending her a stinging reminder now. She was a married woman. Indeed, she was now a married woman with a child. Her husband's child. A good man such as Hugh would never think that that child had been conceived by force. Force against a woman was not an action that Hugh would understand. No, she had come here today to speak to her good friend, Marion. Hugh, and all the bubbling feelings he produced in Margory could no longer be a part of her life.

As though reading her thoughts, a smiling Marion appeared in the doorway of their cottage with Jacob and, walking quickly to Margory, she embraced her.

"How delighted I am that you have been able to come to see me today, Margory." And, lifting the little boy,

"Give my good friend a kiss, Jacob. It's because this lady, whose name is Margory, was so clever when you were born that you're the beautiful boy you are today. Abner, I think you and Hugh should leave Margory and I to have a good talk – women's talk."

Laughing, Abner turned to Hugh who hadn't taken his eyes off Margory the entire time.

"You're right, my dear. Why are women always right, Hugh? I hope to see you again and soon, Margory. In the meantime, I'll leave you and my good wife to gossip. Come, Hugh." Kissing his wife and son and with Hugh clearly reluctant to leave,

"I'm so pleased to have seen you, Margory. And looking as well as ever."

"Come inside, Margory, or these two men will never leave us in peace!"

Chapter 49

"Marion. Why was Hugh here? Did he know that I was coming to see you?"

"No, my dear. I was going to tell Abner this morning when we were breaking our fast, but Jacob was being particularly mischievous and it completely left my mind. What is your concern, my friend? Come, let us take a small ale. It looks to me as though you have a great deal to tell me."

"Perceptive as ever, Marion. How very pleased I am to have such a good friend to whom I can speak in absolute confidence."

"Oh, it's as serious as that, is it? Well, of course, you know that whatever you tell me will go no further. But first, your health. I hope that you are not about to tell me that you are unwell, Margory."

"Not at all, Marion. It's kind of you to ask, but you need have no concern in that area. I am very well and have been so since the birth of my baby five months ago."

"My dear girl. I had heard rumours that you may have had a child. However, as I knew that your husband had treated you so very badly and, indeed, that you were beginning to care for Hugh, I thought the gossip must be wrong – as it often is; you and I know that more than most people. Congratulations, Margory. I am so very happy for you, knowing how much you adore babies and how much you have always wanted your own. I know, too, of course, that dealing with the births of other women's babes, while giving you so much pleasure doing such a good job, it has, at the same time, made you want your own even more. I have always admired you in so many ways, but one of those ways was that you were never envious of other women having babies. You simply wanted your own so very much.

But, in view of the way Arthur treated you, it seemed that it would be almost impossible. I know there are many women much weaker than you are who, given your personal circumstances of your husband leaving and setting up home with another woman, having defrauded your dear parents, would have succumbed to another man for whom their true and honourable feelings were growing. Of course, you were brought up in the true faith to believe that, once your marriage vows have been taken, none could tear them from you. However, I know of no-one, and I mean no-one, who would have blamed you, had you progressed your feelings for Hugh. And I only had to look at his face today to know that he cares for you deeply, Margory."

"Please, Marion, I don't wish to speak to you about Hugh except to say that he is a very dear person but a person I must forget."

"Do tell me, Margory, what it is you were wanting to speak to me about today."

"You are right in saying, Marion, that there is no future for Hugh and me. Indeed, since the birth of Henry, I have no room in my heart for anyone else. He is my whole life. And that's in spite of the way he was conceived. Why, I have even forgotten to arrange his baptism, but am glad to say that it will be next week."

Margory took out a handkerchief.

"My dear. What do you mean by 'the way he was conceived'?"

"Marion. Arthur is a very bad person. First, he not only defrauded my father – and I thank the Lord that neither of my parents ever knew that he had taken, not only their land but that of my grandparents - he built a house far away from here and took in a young woman to bear his children. He then proceeded to lose all that money. That was why he returned to Hertfordshire, to The Manor, saying he was its

Lord. He then proceeded to claim his conjugal rights, whether I wanted him to or no. And I did not want him to – at all. Not for one moment."

"Margory. Are you saying that he forced himself upon you? That he raped you?"

"Perhaps I should have simply given myself to him, Marion. After all, I previously wished to marry him – for all the wrong reasons, of course – and that blame lies entirely with me. And, having married him and longed to lie with him to produce a child, that didn't happen. Nevertheless, I was his wife. I am still his wife in the eyes of the church. It is to my dishonour that, in my husband's absence of four years, I discovered feelings for another man that were wrong of me to harbour. And it is due to those immoral feelings, combined with the fact that I have not cared for Arthur for a very long time that, on my husband's return and claiming his place in my bed, that I refused. I absolutely refused, Marion. I had no wish whatsoever to be coupled with him. So he had no alternative but to force me. I shall not describe to you, Marion, the absolute horror of that episode. Suffice to say that it was the worst experience I have ever had in my entire life of 25 years. Added to that experience is his day-to-day treatment of me. He belittles me, both when we are alone and in front of the servants. But the worst part of this is yet to come, Marion."

"How can anything be worse than what you have just described to me, Margory. He clearly treats you very badly indeed. But he loves his son, does he not?"

Margory took a sip of her drink and said nothing.

"Margory. You must tell me. Are you saying that he not only mistreats you but also your baby? Surely not. If so, he is an even bigger bully and coward than you are allowing me to hear."

"He has only hit Henry once."

"He hit him! When was this?"

"When he was only a matter of weeks old. What you must understand, Marion, is that Arthur doesn't love Henry. Henry merely represents an heir to him, so allowing Arthur to climb another rung of the social ladder. I must hasten to add, Marion, that it was I, in my foolish youth, who introduced Arthur to the clambering of that ladder. It was I who suggested that he joined my family at our end of the dining table. And, when father suggested that I teach Arthur reading, writing and arithmetic, I couldn't have been happier. He was beginning to be included in my family's life and that was exactly what I wanted, then. My mother did try to warn me. Arthur's mother tried to warn me. But I intended to have Arthur. Nothing and nobody was going to stand in my way. I am not proud of my behaviour at that time, Marion."

"Margory. Youth and wisdom do not usually go hand in hand. We learn from our mistakes, hopefully. You are criticising yourself for actions that you took several years ago. We are talking about today. In particular, we are talking about not only your safety but that of your child."

"I care not for my own safety…"

"But I do, Margory. You are confiding in me…"

"And what, pray, is my dear wife confiding in you?"

Chapter 50

Arthur's entrance so startled both women that it took a few minutes for them to recover. Marion was the first to speak,

"I didn't hear you knock, Master Arthur."

"Oh didn't you? Excuse me." With that, he walked out again, closed the door, knocked and walked in.

"I think we should go, Arthur."

"Do you really, wife? We shall leave when I say so. Mistress Marion, your friend is taking a very long time to realise that I shall not be commanded by any woman. We shall leave when one of you has told me what my wife has been confiding. I am perfectly happy to wait all day, if need be. And when you have told me what you have been confiding, Margory, you will tell me why you have been meeting Hugh behind my back. You haven't looked as happy as you did this morning when I was leaving, so I thought I would find out the reason. Now I know there were two. The first was to meet your good friend, Hugh – or was he more than that? No, don't interrupt me, wife. The second was to spread your lies abroad to Marion here."

"I cannot sit here while you insult my dear friend, Master Arthur. She has never lied and I doubt very much that she lies now. Why should she? She was brought up by good parents, she has always followed God's laws, one of which is "Thou Shalt Not Bear False Witness" and, in your absence of four years, she totally understood that she remained your wife. She could, at any time, have decided to ignore her marriage vows as she had no idea where you were or what you were doing and…"

"That's quite enough, Mistress Marion. I can see why my wife chose you as her friend as you are just as commanding as she. Is there no woman who does her husband's bidding any longer…"

"What's going on here? Is that you, Master Arthur? I haven't seen you for, what, more than four years. What has brought about this return?"

"That is no concern of yours, Master Abner. My wife and I shall leave now as I am clearly not going to discover the reason for her visit to Brockminster. We shall take our leave and, if she refuses to tell me on our return to The Manor, I shall beat her in front of our son. In that way, he will find out who is in charge in our household. I'm not surprised that The Manor is so disorganised, as it appears you come running to Brockminster the moment my back is turned."

"This is the first time I have seen my good friend, Marion, in a long time."

"Well, it will be the last time for a long time, so don't expect any more confidences in the near future, Mistress Marion."

Dragging Margory by her arm, he pulled her out of the door and told her to re-mount and stay close by him on their return to The Manor.

"This isn't the last you'll hear from us, Master Arthur."

"I suggest you consider carefully any future actions as it will be your good friend, Margory, who suffers for any further steps you take. And so that she knows I shall not tolerate this sort of behaviour, I shall also beat our son."

At those words, Margory burst into tears, leaned forward and bade her horse to begin the journey home.

Chapter 51

"I had absolutely no idea that I would see Hugh."

"And what, pray, were you confiding in your friend that stopped the moment I entered?"

Margory's scream as Arthur beat her once more was his answer. It didn't matter what Margory said, Arthur just did not believe that she had bumped into Hugh unexpectedly. That aside, of course, Arthur insisted on knowing what she had confided to Marion. Although she told him, she covered just the bare bones of her chat to Marion and Arthur didn't believe that either. Somehow, from somewhere, he had acquired a cane and proceeded to take both Margory and Henry to the bedchamber. She implored Arthur to give her a double dose of beating and to spare Henry. But the more she wept, the more he beat the little fellow who had cried for several hours after Arthur had put the cane away. He then left on the journey he had intended to take that morning, making Margory promise on the Bible that she would not leave the house and grounds. He needn't have elicited that promise as she didn't intend to risk Henry getting another beating. The next one would have been the end of the baby who could no longer crawl around. Neither was he seen to smile for a very long time. In fact, a change had come over him which, to start with, wasn't really noticed.

Chapter 52

Truth to tell, although Arthur had intended to beat Margory and Henry in a way that Margory would never forget, once he had started, a madness seemed to overtake him as he thought back to his beloved Hannah. His Hannah who had died of neglect, taking their unborn baby with her to the grave. He had never loved before Hannah and he had not loved since. Lucy had been the one he had chosen to run his estate in North West England, purely because she looked so much like Hannah, they could have been sisters. But Lucy hadn't replaced Hannah in his heart. When Hannah had died, he had considered killing Margory and, on several occasions, was close to doing just that. But he didn't intend to be executed or spend the rest of his days in prison. Unless, of course, he could claim self-defence under the 1532 law. No, what he did intend was to take his revenge somehow. So instead, he had gradually and meticulously siphoned off all earnings from Margory's parents' land. He hadn't been sure what he would do with the money or when he would do it, but then Margory's parents had been put to the stake and that was his moment. He was never sure whether he would have deceived Margory's father, had he lived, as he had always liked the old man. So it suited his plan well when they were no longer around. He cared not at all that Margory was left penniless. She did, after all, have a small inheritance from her mother that he couldn't touch, so she wasn't entirely without income. When he had considered it at all – which he hadn't very often - he had actually thought that she might sell the family estate to a rich landowner who could afford to get the land working again and re-build The Manor. Instead, she had started working as a midwife in Brockminster and had accepted Lord Winchester's help to regain the estate's former glory. Arthur had occasionally travelled South, gossiped at the local inn and been told that Margory seemed to be getting to know the man who was re-building her estate. Indeed, he had been told that Hugh Taylor was a customer at the inn when working at The Manor. Oh yes, he knew about her so-called friendship with the man. However, unfortunately, and in spite of ale-laden tongues, he could never find someone who thought their relationship had gone further than friendship. If it had, his use of the whip and birch could have been a daily occurrence. Alternatively, he could have thrown her out of The Manor. He could then have lived his lordly life exactly as he wished. Although he didn't go to church, Arthur was sure that adultery was one of the ten commandments so it was more than likely that this Hugh Taylor and Margory had only pursued a relationship outside the bedchamber. Pity. On the other hand, if his wife was now meeting the man secretly… Yes, he would watch his wife's movements. It had been a good idea of his to pay one of the stable lads to watch her, too, when he was at the inn or away. He didn't want her visiting her so-called friends in Brockminster. In fact, he didn't want Margory at The Manor at all. After all, if he wanted a woman he could take Lucy – or one of the servants who took his fancy. And now there was the pretty, young midwife. But his son and heir must stay. After all, he was Lord of the Manor. He would ensure that no-one forgot it.

Chapter 53

Margory could barely move, but move she did, painfully, slowly, between her bed and Henry's crib. Caring not whether Arthur found out, she sent for the family physician who said that, while there were no broken bones, the child would need to rest and he would tell the apothecary to send appropriate ointment. When he asked how the injuries had been sustained, Margory didn't reply. All she said was that she needed to recover fully in order to take good care of her child. At that, the doctor had given her a penetrating look and nodded.

Arthur returned and left again. How many times, Margory didn't know and didn't care. She wished he would go away and stay away, but she knew that wouldn't happen. Week in, week out, Margory tended her child, tenderly bathing him, comforting and cuddling him until, gradually, when she placed him gently on the floor, he had begun to move along, little by little, but not sitting as that made him scream in pain. But he persisted until, one day, he had rolled over into a sitting position and, although his brows furrowed momentarily, he gave Margory such a sunny smile that she wept with joy. At that very moment, Arthur had entered the bedchamber and Henry had looked at him with widening eyes. This was a look Margory had never seen him give anyone in the past. Looking from son to father, Margory saw Arthur clutch his buttocks and yell so loudly, she was astonished and puzzled.

"What ails you, Arthur?"

"I must have ridden too hard and long. I shall retire to one of the other bedchambers and summon Lucy. Why is that child laughing?"

Yet another surprise. Although Margory delighted in Henry's increasing number of smiles, she had never heard him or any other child of his age laugh out loud, as he was doing now. But it was such an infectious laugh that Margory had to turn her head away in order to contain her own bubbling mirth.

"I'm sure he isn't laughing at your discomfort, Arthur. He's only a baby."

"Yes, well, if he laughs at my pain again, he'll wish he hadn't."

Margory struggled to her feet and picked up Henry who nuzzled into her neck. He then turned and, looking Margory in the eye, he laughed again. Margory knew that different babies developed at different rates, but Henry was a little young to be doing more than smiling. How puzzling. But it was such a pleasure to see his little face light up that she smiled back at him, at which he again snuggled into her love.

Chapter 54

"Oh, who can that be at this early hour? I still have a great deal to do in preparation for Henry's baptism."

"Your ladyship. The midwife is waiting to see you in the library."

"The midwife? I wasn't aware of her visit today. Goodwife Sykes, would you please finish bathing Henry. I've put out his baptism clothes. Would you ensure that James has sufficient Hippocras in the cellar for a small gathering following the baptism. I must speak to the midwife as it is very inconvenient for her to simply arrive, unannounced."

"Good morning, Mistress Turner. I wasn't aware…"

"You needn't trouble yourself, wife. I did know of Mistress Turner's visit and of course I told you. Oh dear, yet another example, my dear, of my wife's increasing mental difficulty."

"I have no…"

"Come. As you can see, my wife is well – other than her mental problems, of course, which I shall have to deal with. But for the moment, it isn't necessary for you to see our son. Come, let us be away in the carriage, as I promised."

"Arthur. Have you yourself forgotten that today is an important day? Our son is to be baptised and I shall need the carriage."

"You do see what I mean, Mistress Turner? To start with, and as I understand it, this baptism should have been done some time ago. Also, I knew nothing of its being arranged for today. What a shame that I, the father, cannot be present."

"But surely, Arthur…"

"Wife. I will hear nothing further. I knew nothing of this baptism and I think it to be most ungracious for this lady to be inconvenienced by sending her away. No. She and I will take a ride in the carriage so you, the babe and the servants will have to walk. It is, indeed, a pity that it is raining hard but I do not intend to break my promise to this lady midwife. Good day. I am unsure when I shall be returning, but when I do, you and I shall discuss your mental health as it appears to be deteriorating. I am becoming increasingly concerned that you are not a fit mother for the son of the Lord of the Manor. Perhaps you need to be housed elsewhere. Come Beth…er…Mistress Turner. Let us make haste to the carriage as I wouldn't want your pretty little feet to get wet."

Chapter 55

"Sir, are you sure you should be making your wife and baby walk in this torrential rain? Perhaps I should visit on another day…"

"Nonsense. I have arranged for you to visit today. Had I known about my son's baptism, I would have changed its date as I think it is important for you to keep a watchful eye on my son. One of these days you may arrive, only to find that he has been dropped once again and bones have been broken. It is essential that you watch over my son."

"Yes, of course, your Lordship. That is what I wish to do…"

"Then let me hear nothing further about it. My carriage awaits. Let me help you inside. I'm sure you have never had the privilege of riding in a carriage, have you? I have had this one imported specially from Hungary. If you sit close to me, you will find it more comfortable." Arthur rapped on the roof and the carriage moved away.

"Oh, your Lordship, I don't think her Ladyship would like your hand to be there."

"No, but I do, and if you are hoping to be licensed, you will need to get used to my hand enjoying your lovely body. And as for those lips. What a very pretty lady you are, Beth."

"Here we are at the inn. I shall take your arm so that you don't slip in the mud. Let us secure a seat away from the crowds where I may get to know you better."

Chapter 56

"Oh, Goodwife Sykes, I am so sorry that you have had to walk to the church."

"Don't you worry about me, m'lady. I'm just pleased that you were able to wrap the little one so that he isn't drenched. I noticed when I was bathing him this morning that he is a brave little fellow when water is splashed on his face – doesn't mind at all.

"Yes, he's perfectly dry, I'm pleased to say. But you must rest when we return to The Manor as you are wet through. I can't tell you how very annoyed I am that my husband insisted on using the carriage on such a day. I know that I told him of the baptism."

"Never you mind, your Ladyship. We're inside at last, with your friends to greet us, I believe. And isn't that master Taylor?"

Margory's heart leapt in a mixture of apprehension and delight; what if Arthur were to find out. At the same time, it was always such a pleasure to see Hugh's kind face. Turning to Goodwife Sykes,

"I had no idea that Master Taylor would be joining us, Goodwife Sykes, and I do not wish my husband to find out." Patting Margory's arm reassuringly, she nodded.

"Knowing you as I do, Mistress, you need have no concern there." Then, turning to the others, Margory said,

"Thank you so much for agreeing to be Henry's Godparents, Marion and Abner. He should, of course, have another Godfather, but I haven't been able to arrange that. Hugh. While I am always happy to see you, I wasn't aware of your coming to Henry's baptism and, should my husband find out, both Henry and I will suffer as Arthur doesn't believe anything I say."

"Don't you worry, my dear, I only came to ensure for myself that you and your son are well. I happened to see Arthur earlier at the inn with a young woman. I know that he didn't see me. I shall take my leave now."

The Priest approached and took Henry, first anointing him with oils followed by blessed water being poured over his head three times. Henry jumped a little when the first lot of water was poured, but then gave one of his enigmatic smiles which seemed to surprise the Priest a little. As the baptism drew to a close, Marion took Henry and realised that his swaddling bands needed to be changed.

"Margory, I'll take the bands and change Henry while you stay here and talk to Abner. Father Antonio, would you show me, please, where it will be convenient for me to clean little Henry. Thank you."

"Oh, thank you, Marion. That would be really helpful."

Chapter 57

"Where's Henry, Marion?"

Kissing Margory on the cheek, Marion whispered,

"Do you trust me, Margory?"

"You know that I trust you implicitly, Marion. At the same time, my dear son is rarely out of my sight, so I'm concerned."

"It distresses me to say this, Margory, but, in order that you tell Arthur truthfully that you don't know where Henry is, it is better that I don't tell you. But, Margory, it is really important that you trust me when I tell you that Henry is totally safe and well looked after. Once he has fully recovered from Arthur's latest beating, he won't experience another. That is what you want, isn't it."

"Yes, of course, you know it is. At the same time…Not to know where my baby son is…How can I bear that? And how shall I explain his absence and the fact that I have returned without him?"

"This is what you're going to say, Margory."

As Marion began to tell Margory how Henry's absence would be explained, and in spite of the fact that Margory knew her friend very well, liked her very much and did trust her, her tears grew large and threatened to spill. Seeing her dear friend upset, Marion hugged her. Again, speaking softly, she said,

"My dear Margory, always remember that it is Henry's welfare that you want to be safeguarded, and that I would never participate in any action that would harm him. I'm only sorry that it is important for you not to know so that you can remain the truthful person you are and always have been."

"But where is Henry now, Marion? Is he still in the church? I would like to say a temporary farewell. Oh Marion, I don't know whether I can do this."

"No, Margory. He is no longer here. And, in any case, that would not be wise, as I'm sure you realise. I'm so sorry, but what you and I both know is that Henry must be kept safe from harm."

And, of course, Margory wanted that more than anything else in the world. But how could she bear to be without her darling baby.

Chapter 58

Although the sun was shining when Margory and the servants returned to The Manor, she thought that she had never felt so very sad. Goodwife Sykes had been the first to ask,

"Are you well, your Ladyship? Where is Henry?" This was Margory's first test.

"I don't know. The last time I saw and held him was when he was being baptised. I'll tell you when we get back to The Manor and I've spoken to Master Arthur."

Margory went into the library and sat down. She needed to think things through. First, of course, she trusted her good friend, Marion, implicitly. Secondly, how would she live through each day without seeing her baby? The thought was abhorrent. On the other hand, she would not have to face seeing him beaten to within an inch of his life by Arthur…

"Yes, what is it? Can I not have two moments alone without being disturbed? Yes, Lucy?"

"Mistress, his Lordship left a message for me to give you."

"A message? I was just about to speak to him myself."

"He said to tell you that he has had to go away for a few days and has taken the carriage. He said he wanted to show the midwife where he intends to buy another property in the North West of the country."

Margory gazed at Lucy who lowered her eyes. Both were thinking back all those years when it had been Lucy who had accompanied Arthur to somewhere in another part of England. Arthur hadn't changed and he never would.

"I see. Please tell Goodwife Sykes that I would like all the servants to gather in the main kitchen right away."

"Yes, mistress. I'm so…"

"Please do as I ask, Lucy – now – and let me know when everyone has gathered."

It was many years since Lucy had heard agitation in Margory's voice so, turning quickly, she left, closing the library door softly behind her.

Chapter 59

"I have asked you all to gather together so that I may tell you some extremely sad news."

The chattering ceased immediately as the servants looked at their mistress expectantly.

"My darling boy has been abducted."

A whoosh of gasping went through the throng.

"I have done all that can be done under these dreadful circumstances. Lord Winchester, the judge in Brockminster, who is a good family friend, has alerted two of his constables who are searching, first Greenwillows, then Brockminster and, if necessary, further afield, throughout the county. Tomorrow I shall ride to Brockminster Hall to ask his Lordship if anything more can be done. In the meantime, I would ask all of you to be vigilant at this very sorrowful time. Please keep your eyes open for anything unusual in case it should be an indication of where my dear child is. However, as you can imagine, I am extremely upset and don't know how I can bear not seeing Henry. I shall retire to the library and do not wish to be disturbed, unless it is to be told news of my boy's disappearance or something else of extreme importance. Is that understood?"

Nodding of heads greeted this request and Goodwife Sykes stepped forward. As always, she was the thoughtful spokesperson for the servants.

"Your Ladyship. I'm sure you realise that when you are hurt, we are all hurt. We shall leave you to your thoughts, knowing that if you need anything – anything at all – you will summon us. We shall, of course, do as you ask, and be vigilant regarding anything that may shed light on where your son is. Please know, too, that you will be in our daily prayers."

"As always, Goodwife Sykes, you are extremely helpful and I know that I can count on the help of all of you."

Chapter 60

Margory's body was moving of its own accord and her feet took her, as they so often had, into the library, the door of which her hands closed softly. She was totally unaware of what she was doing and that large tears were falling down her cheeks, nor did she care. Her beautiful baby boy was no longer here to stare at the wet, rolling object that he had witnessed too many times. On those occasions, his little face had echoed his mother's sadness and his fat, tiny finger had prodded the tear. In such a short time, he had shared his mother's distress as well as her joy.

Pressing the button that opened the small door, Margory crouched into what was usually her haven of peace. But even this secret sanctuary was peaceful no more. With the loss of her precious child, her heart had been torn from her body and her whole being felt numb.

"Please Lord, guide me down the path of knowing what I should do. I beg of you, too, to numb this powerful pain that is subsuming me. How can I live, day by day, without seeing my dear child? Please keep him safe and happy, under the protection of my good friend, Marion. I thank you for that."

Stooping to leave, there was a soft knock on the door.

Opening it, "I did ask not to be disturbed. What is it?"

"I'm very sorry, your Ladyship, it is Mistress Marion."

"Oh, I'm sorry to have spoken sharply, I'll show her in myself. Thank you."

"Dear Marion, this is a lovely surprise. Do come in."

"I do apologise for not asking if it was convenient for me to visit, Margory. It was simply that I wanted to see for myself how you're getting on. It was a last minute decision."

"Come into the library, Marion." Then, ringing the bell,

"Goodwife Sykes. Please ask James to serve refreshments for us in the library as Mistress Marion has arrived unexpectedly."

"Thank you, Margory, but a small ale will suffice as I can't stay long."

Taking her friend in a warm embrace, Margory said,

"If I had to choose who I would like to visit me at the moment, Marion, it would be you, so please don't worry that I didn't know about your visit."

As they sat down, Margory burst into tears at the same time as Goodwife Sykes entered with the drinks.

"Oh, Mistress Margory, I'm so sorry to interrupt when you are upset."

"I'm afraid you and the staff may have to become accustomed to seeing me in this troubled state. In fact, this is one occasion – against gossip as I am, as you know – that it will be helpful for you to tell everyone here that my tears may become commonplace at the moment."

Chapter 61

With glazed eyes and speaking quietly, Margory asked,

"How is my dear boy, Marion? Is he well? I can't begin to describe how much I miss him."

"Yes, of course you do, Margory. You wouldn't be a normal mother if you didn't. He is, of course, totally safe, but, as you realise, it is better that I don't tell you where he is. But tell me, what was Arthur's reaction when you told him of the abduction?"

"I returned to be told that my husband had made a short visit with the midwife, with whom he has gone away for several days. There was a time, Marion, when that would have distressed me – but no longer. Leopards don't change their spots any more than Arthur will ever change. What he will do when he returns, I don't know. No doubt I shall be blamed for not being sufficiently watchful. However, I care not. He can now no longer beat Henry in order to make me suffer – and for that I thank you."

"Tell me, Margory. Is someone keeping watch here – for someone or something? I thought I saw someone behind the bushes as I arrived. But when I glanced in that direction, they moved away."

"How strange. But I don't think it's anything to do with what Arthur believes to be Henry's abduction because I have also felt that someone was watching me."

"Shall I tell you what I think, Margory? I think that Arthur has told one of his servants to make sure that you don't see Hugh."

"Marion. That is entirely possible, but hadn't crossed my mind at all. Certainly, at the moment, there is no room in my mind for anything other than not seeing my dear boy. But thank you for mentioning that, Marion. I'll watch out. But at least Arthur won't have the pleasure of being told that I'm seeing Hugh – because, of course, I'm not, sadly. To be perfectly honest, Marion, I've been so very upset about Henry's absence that Hugh has rarely entered my mind at all. If Arthur has done as you suggest, and told one of the servants to see if Hugh visits, he will be disappointed. However, I shall keep what you say in mind."

"Surely Arthur won't take offence at my visiting you, Margory? Why should he?"

"No, I don't think so. Only insofar as Hugh and Abner are friends and Arthur may think that you're carrying messages to me from Hugh."

"Oh, I hadn't thought of that! Perhaps I could do that!"

"No, Marion, definitely not. The worry of not seeing my dear boy is more than enough. I certainly don't intend to give Arthur reason to suspect that, in addition to my not being able to take proper care of our son, that I am also seeing another man. No. At the moment, I have no idea what Arthur's reaction will be to Henry's abduction on his return. But I am sure to be blamed. As I am blamed for everything else that goes wrong in this household. And, indeed, he tells others that I am losing my mind, so this will be yet another reason for him to continue to defame me to others. It concerns me where this will end."

"I'm so pleased that we have had this chat, Margory, as I can now see that Arthur must be watched even more than I had suspected."

Chapter 62

The door burst open and in strode Arthur, a big grin lighting his face in a way that Margory hadn't seen for some time. The grin disappeared on seeing Marion.

"And what, may I ask, are you doing here? Invited by my wife, no doubt, in my absence…"

"Not at all, Master Arthur. I took the decision to visit my friend without telling her, in the hope that she would be at home."

"Well. I'm not surprised that you're her friend as you seem to have no manners, as neither does she."

"I beg your pardon, sir, but knowing Margory as I do, and being the good, long-standing friend that she is, I knew that, if she were in residence on my arrival, she would tell me if my visit was not convenient. That is the essence of our friendship."

"That may be the foundation of your friendship, but you and I are not friends and it is most inconvenient for me that you are here. Please leave."

Margory and Marion embraced and, with an icy stare, Marion went into the hall where Goodwife Sykes, having been summoned by Margory, brought her cape.

"Goodbye, my dear. I shall visit again, but next time, I shall let you know beforehand."

"…which is the usual, good mannered way to behave, mistress. Good day to you. And when you do visit, ensure that neither your husband nor your husband's friend accompany you. If you ignore my command, your friend, Margory, will suffer, as will our son. By the way, where is Henry?"

Chapter 63

"Let us return to the library, husband, so that I may tell you some very sad news."

"What is it, woman? I've no time for sitting around. I'm about to go to the inn. Quick. It's sure to be nothing of interest to me. What is it? Some domestic difficulty you can't handle as the lady of the manor should be able to do? You've certainly got enough staff to do your bidding. Some time soon, I shall take a look at each and every one of those servants as some are too old to remain and some are not doing the job they were hired to do. Dear God, what is it?"

"Our dear son has…"

"Stop your wailing, woman. Where is Henry?"

"I don't know…"

"What do you mean, 'you don't know'. He's my son and heir. You have a responsibility to know exactly where he is, when. Is this yet another failing. Are you not capable of keeping him safe at all?"

Tears of frustration drowned Margory's face.

"He has been abducted…"

"Abducted! Good God, woman. Are you telling me that, as well as losing your mind, you have lost our son? What kind of mother are you? How did it happen and where?"

Knocking on the door.

"Is there nowhere I can be at peace in my own home. Yes, Goodwife Sykes?"

"A rider has just left a message addressed to you, Master Arthur."

"A rider? Message? Who was the rider? Why didn't you find out? I can see that I must get rid of those servants who are too old to do a good job. And soon."

Ripping open the message, Arthur bellowed:

"£100! I'm being asked for £100 for the return of my son. Well, that little beast who laughed when I was in pain isn't worth £10 never mind £100. I can buy several stables of fine horses for much less than that amount – and would gain much more enjoyment than from that scrap of humanity. He can stay where he is with whomever he is lodging. You and I will simply have to create another heir, wife. I care not for the return of my son. Now I shall go to the inn where we shall have a good laugh at this demand for £100. This latest forgetfulness of yours, wife, is worrying. I shall need to continue seeking alternative accommodation for you. I've been looking into the Hospital of St Mary of Bethlehem but they charge a fee so I shall think again."

Margory's thoughts were with this latest development of the demand for £100, so the possibility of being put into Bedlam did not immediately catch her attention.

"What else does it say, Arthur? Do they say what will happen if you don't give them the money?"

Arthur read the note again.

"Oh yes. A rider will be despatched in one week's time for the money. If it isn't given to him, we shall not see the child again. Well, that makes no difference to me. I certainly won't be parting with £100. Babes are easily made. I've lost count of how many I've created. But, of course, they're illegitimate so can't inherit my fine manor house and land as I intend. Yes, you and I will be coming together again, wife, even if I have to force you again. Enough of this. I'm off to see what the folk at the inn have to say. I'll take sixpence for a willing woman although I have to say that it isn't as much fun as when I have to force you into submission. I know not when I shall return as I shall take the coach north for several days. I've been playing Primero with a great deal of luck lately and shall soon be in a position to buy another property there. I'm also meeting some highly influential people."

Margory turned away. Arthur's reaction to gaining another heir didn't surprise her at all. What she didn't like was his suggestion that the creation of another child would, once more, be dealt with by force. She would need to think about this, and in the meantime, she would pray for guidance.

Chapter 64

Anxiety knitted Hugh's brow:

"I can't stand by and do nothing, Abner. Although Margory, Marion, you and I know that Henry is safe, Margory will be suffering deeply without her baby boy. Not only that, Henry himself is clearly upset without his mother – and that's in spite of the fact that he enjoys playing with Jacob. The three of us must meet to discuss what can be done."

"What we do know, though, Hugh, is that you can't be seen anywhere near Margory or she will be subjected to yet another beating. Although Margory is comforted by the fact that her child can no longer be harmed, I'm not sure how long she can endure the sort of physical pain that Arthur metes out. From what Marion tells me, Arthur is also undermining her confidence regularly and making it appear to outsiders that she's losing her mind. Such is the way of tyrants. It may be that he has a plan to send her away so that he can live the life he wishes. As The Manor is, of course, Margory's home and has been in her family for several generations, that can't be allowed to happen, in spite of the fact that, once they were married, it became Arthur's property, of course. Once Marion, you and I have talked through what our next step is, I think it may be wise for one of us to speak to Lord Winchester. As a judge, a good man and a friend of, not only Margory's, but her late parents, too, I'm sure he will have good advice that we can act upon."

Chapter 65

Margory's feet seemed to have a mind of their own. Once again, she found herself kneeling before the secret, small altar of Our Lady, praying for guidance.

"Dear Lord, I know not which way to turn. I have no idea what to do next. Thank you for keeping my dear child safe, as I know he is. However, my heart breaks without his presence and I know that he must be very sad without me, too. Please Lord, don't allow him to think that I have forsaken him as this may affect his mind and emotions adversely, not only now but in the future. But no, Marion assured me that she would speak of me every day so that his fire of love remains burning brightly. Please clothe him in your own, dear love. I shall ask Marion to make sure that I am included in Henry's daily prayers, as he is in mine."

Returning to the library, a soft knock preceded Goodwife Sykes' entering,

"Mistress Margory, this is a busy day for messages. Yet another, this time for your good self."

"Thank you, Goodwife Sykes. I shall read this alone."

"My dear friend. You will know what I mean when I say that all is well here. I thought you would want to know that news has come to our attention that your cousin Elizabeth has been arrested in Essex, accused of witchcraft. However, it sounds as though her sister, Agnes, is in more serious difficulties as she has admitted that she is a witch. We were told that Agnes's daughter, Joan, has also been arrested. In view of your own extremely distressing experience of being accused of witchcraft, I thought you may wish to go to Essex to support your cousin and, perhaps, also, speak to Agnes Waterhouse. Please let me know if you would like to do this because, if so, Abner and I will accompany you.

Abner will, of course, need to ask Lord Winchester's permission to accompany you. I shall await your reply."

Not requiring a second bidding, Margory summoned Goodwife Sykes and told her to tell Thomas to prepare her horse as she was going away for a few days.

"Master Arthur has gone North for several days so it won't be necessary for you to tell him that I have gone."

Margory held Goodwife Sykes's eye in such a way that the old woman knew exactly what her mistress meant.

"Ruth will accompany me as she enjoys riding and is also perfectly discreet. It would be helpful to me if you would engage Thomas in the kitchen. Perhaps cook could tempt him with his favourite sweetmeat?"

Once again, Goodwife Sykes nodded, knowing exactly her mistress's intention. They both smiled. In the midst of heartbreak, Margory again felt the welling warmth of friendship for her staff, in particular Goodwife Sykes.

Chapter 66

Once again, Margory thrilled to the feel of the wind in her hair as she and Ruth flew across the countryside. As they neared Marion's cottage, Margory held her breath. Would she see Hugh again? As Marion and Abner came out to greet her, Margory wasn't sure whether she felt disappointment or relief when she saw that Hugh was not there. Perhaps he was no longer interested in a woman who not only lived with her husband but had had a child by him, too. No, Margory must try very hard to forget Hugh. But she wasn't sure she could do that.

"Dear Margory. I knew you would want to see your relatives as you, of all people, know the dreadful distress they will be going through. However, from what I hear, Agnes Waterhouse has admitted to being a witch. Perhaps that is just rumour as she will know the consequences. We thought you would want to speak to her yourself in prison. However, in view of your own past, our judge, Lord Winchester, on being asked by Abner if he could accompany you to Essex, said that he would accompany us, too, as it would be dangerous for you to visit Agnes and Elizabeth in prison on your own. Where accusations of witchcraft are concerned, many take the law into their own hands. Also Lord Winchester's carriages are very comfortable." Marion smiled.

"Where is…?"

"I knew, of course, that you would want to see Henry. But do you really think that to be a good idea, Margory? Having a little one of my own, I do know, dear friend, what you are going through during this time of not seeing your lovely son. However, if you see him and he you, I doubt that wild horses could pull you apart. This is your decision, Margory, but do give it a little thought."

Margory thought her heart would burst, not only for love of her child but because she missed him so very much. Little ones changed and developed so quickly. What was he doing now that he wasn't doing when she was observing him every day? How could she bear to miss those changes? Perhaps she could remain hidden by a tree and watch him playing with Jacob for a while. But could she risk his seeing her? His wonderful eyes had never missed anything. If that happened, she knew that he would cling closely and never let her go. No, she must be strong. As tears threatened, she joined her friend again.

"As always, you are quite right, Marion. I miss dear little Henry so much that I feel bodily pain at not being able to hold him close. But I'm an adult and he's a child, so I must not succumb to my own weakness. Let us depart quickly, Marion, before I change my mind and decide that I cannot bear to be without him one moment longer. Who will be caring for him and Jacob while we are in Essex?"

"A good friend of mine who has two children of her own is with Henry and Jacob now and they will stay with her until our return."

Chapter 67

Lord Winchester gently guided Margory to a quiet spot.

"Now, my dear, what you must realise is that this trial is a very important one. So important, in fact, that the Queen's own Attorney General, Sir Gilbert Gerard, as well as John Southcote, Justice of the Queen's Bench, will be present for the second examination. In order to ensure that you will be perfectly safe when visiting both Agnes Waterhouse and Elizabeth, your cousin, whom I suggest you visit first, I have spoken to Sir Gilbert. What I would advise, my dear, is that at no time should you speak of your religious leanings, and certainly not the fact that you, yourself, was on trial for witchcraft some time ago. When Sir Gilbert is in London, at court, he is, of course, of the Protestant persuasion. You need to take care that you exercise the same diplomacy. Am I making myself clear?"

Margory nodded. Lord Winchester was, once again, proving to be a good, wise friend. Having been brought up by a recusant father, and in spite of loving him dearly, her ultimate wish was to grow old so that she could see her son happy and settled, with a large family of his own. Who knew? Perhaps God may even grant she, herself other children. At the thought, Margory shuddered. Loving children as she did, she would, nevertheless, avoid at all costs being subjugated to the disgust of Arthur's forcing himself upon her. No, she would prefer to end her days with just one child if that was to be the only alternative.

"Margory. Am I making myself clear? You seemed to drift into another world for a moment." Margory shook herself as though returning from afar.

"Yes, of course. Is this the Sir Gilbert Gerard who owns much of Lancashire, Lord Winchester? I believe my husband, Arthur, mentioned him the other day as he had seen him at a particularly pleasant inn. Arthur thought that Sir Gilbert was a very good chess player and that he would like to play as well as he does. Also, during the arrangements for my wedding, mother told me that Sir Gilbert had been invited. I recall her mentioning that, as Hertfordshire was so close to London, he was happy to have the excuse of travelling South as she thought he was helping Princess Elizabeth with something or other before she came to the throne."

"The very same. He has travelled all the way to Chelmsford to ensure that justice is done here. Although, of course, he attends the Queen's court regularly and is of great service to Her Majesty, he also has many distinguished friends, as did your parents. When Sir Gilbert appears, I shall make his presence known to you. It isn't expected that he will stay long, however, as the queen has asked him to return to court so that she is kept fully informed about this event. I believe he will also be present at a Tallis concert prior to his return to Lancashire. I understand, too, that your friend, Elizabeth of Hardwick, is at court at the moment. I won't gossip about her reasons for being at court, as I'm sure she will tell you when you see her next. Suffice to say that she and the Queen are good friends."

"Oh, I wish I had known that she is here. I would have invited her to stay at The Manor, n spite of the fact that it isn't the grand house it was when my parents lived. Thank you for mentioning Bess. If it is convenient, I would like to visit her to ask her advice in the fairly near future."

In fact, it was unnecessary for Sir Gilbert to be drawn to Margory's attention. When he took his place at the trial, his handsome bearing was so imposing that she was immediately impressed by his determined mouth, stylish beard and moustache. On looking around, however, for a moment she thought she saw Hugh mingling in the crowd and her heart leapt. She had quite forgotten the depth of her affection for the dear man. But what was he doing here?

Chapter 68

Margory and her cousin embraced, although Margory was puzzled to see her smiling so broadly.

"Elizabeth. Please tell me why you are being accused of witchcraft. What have you done or said that makes people think that?"

Suddenly, Margory's past came tumbling back. The fear, the horror, the lies others told, lying one on top of another, layer after layer, day after day. Gossip. Gossip that knew only one side. Gossip bereft of fairness. Gossip so malicious that it could result in the end of another's life where the noose awaited. Her palms became damp at the memory.

"They've told me I shall be examined first, so I shall tell them this isn't my fault. When I stayed with grandmother, she gave me a cuddly kitten. I loved it, it was my friend. Then, when it was grown, I gave it to Agnes in exchange for a cake. I love cakes."

Margory's own love of cakes, added to her trial for witchcraft, made her move closer to her cousin. The similarity was frightening. Elizabeth continued,

"I used to pretend the cat spoke to me and only me. It was fun and I was lonely! I started thinking up stories about it. I liked sheep as well as my cat. And the sheep liked me! They used to follow me. Then I was told I had stolen them. What's the difference? If a cat and sheep like you, why wouldn't they follow you and why wouldn't you want to keep them? I've been told that if I'm hung it will be the short hang. I don't care. Agnes and Joan are my friends. If they're going to die, I want to die, too. Nobody has ever paid any attention to me before. Now I'm making up these silly stories and suddenly I've got crowds of people around me. Oh, hello Agnes."

Margory could hardly believe her ears. Then she remembered her father saying that Elizabeth and Agnes were very close and whatever Agnes did, Elizabeth copied – and vice versa. But in a way she admired Elizabeth. She wasn't at all frightened of the noose. All she wanted was to be with her sister, whether that was on earth or the other place. She could understand that. After all, she only wanted to be with Henry. She also wanted to be with Hugh, of course, but that was impossible. Had that really been him she saw earlier? In a way she hoped that he didn't care for her still, as they had no future together. But she knew that her longing for him would never die.

"Agnes. This is my cousin, Margory, come all the way from Hertfordshire to speak to me. She was accused of witchcraft several years ago, weren't you Margory?"

"Sssh Elizabeth. That's in the past and it would be better to leave it there."

"All right, but it doesn't matter, does it? Turned out to be a pack of lies, anyway, didn't it, from what I heard? I'm sorry I couldn't get to your trial, but I didn't have any money then and still don't. That's why we're happy to die, Agnes, aren't we. We were nobodies until these silly accusations. Now we're known in most of Essex, you heard about us in Hertfordshire and, best of all, the Queen's Attorney will be hearing our cases. Imagine! The Attorney of Queen Elizabeth herself. I tell you, Margory, we're famous now and we shall die famous. Everyone in history will know that this is the very first execution of a witch, whether that's Agnes or me. It doesn't matter and neither of us cares. We're known everywhere! Agnes is happy that I shall be speaking first and has told me to accuse her of whatever I like. So that's what I shall do." And again, much to Margory's surprise, she smiled broadly.

"Well, I think you're both very brave, and I shall pray that you don't suffer, if either or both of you are declared guilty."

Giving Elizabeth a hug, Margory said her farewells to both women, wishing them well. But after all she had heard, she wasn't very hopeful. Walking down the main street, she looked over at the church of St Mary the Virgin that was in the midst of being re-built. Perhaps if she went in there and prayed, her cousin would be spared.

"Dear Margory. I've been looking everywhere for you. Have you spoken to your cousin? Is she frightened that she'll be accused wrongly, in the way you were?"

Margory jumped. She had been so absorbed and amazed that her cousin appeared perfectly willing to be executed, she hadn't heard Marion coming up behind her. She turned and gazed at her friend as though she was resuming her place on earth after scudding with the clouds.

"No, Marion. It might be better if she was afraid. She seems determined to follow Agnes to the noose. Would you wait there a moment while I go into the church?"

"Of course not, my dear. But I think we should be returning to Brockminster, now that it's getting dark. You and your personal maid will have your onward journey to Greenwillows when we get back, of course. It's beginning to rain, too, so that will slow our return journey."

Entering the church, Margory thought that the weather was echoing her own, miserable thoughts. There had been the occasional time when she had wondered whether she was a witch. Could it be something that her family suffered from?

Chapter 69

July 26th, 1566

At the trial, Elizabeth Francis was examined first. She confessed to possessing the familiar, a white spotted cat named Satan (or Sathan). She said that she had received the cat from her grandmother, Mother Eve of Hatfield Peverell, who taught her witchcraft when she was twelve years old. Elizabeth had kept the cat for fifteen or sixteen years, before eventually giving it to Agnes Waterhouse. According to Elizabeth, the cat spoke to her in a strange, hollow voice and would do anything for her in exchange for a drop of blood. She confessed to stealing sheep, and killing several people including a wealthy man, Andrew Byles, who would not marry her after she became pregnant with his child. She also said the cat instructed her on what herbs to drink to terminate the pregnancy. Later, after she married, she was unhappy and willed the cat to kill her six-month-old daughter and make her husband lame. The confessions that she made expanded the scope of her crimes considerably. Elizabeth was the first to be accused, and was the one who accused Agnes Waterhouse.

Elizabeth told Margory that Agnes would be put on trial the following day, July 27th and that she, too, would be pleading guilty. As Margory intended to return to Hertfordshire that day, July 26th, she told Elizabeth that she would not know the result of that trial for some time. She did, in fact, hear of the execution of Agnes Waterhouse on July 29th, 1566 and, several years later, in 1579, that of her cousin, Elizabeth. She told no-one what Elizabeth had said, nor of her relationship to her.

Chapter 70

"You're very quiet, Margory, my dear. Can I do anything to help?"

"Unfortunately, no-one can, Marion. I'm not sure whether to be glad or sad that we made this journey. I just don't understand how Elizabeth and Agnes can be so willing to risk the noose. And that's not all. Why would they admit to so many terrible acts just so they can become famous and remain together in death? All that is in spite of Elizabeth's having been told that she will probably experience the short hang, if found guilty. It seems more likely that Agnes will be found guilty and that will mean she will be the very first person accused of witchcraft to be executed in this country. They both seem to be treating it as some sort of game of fame."

"Did either of them tell you what they are accused of, Margory?"

Feeling a lump of distress growing in her throat, Margory said,

"Yes, Marion, Elizabeth did, but if you don't mind, I don't feel like talking about it. Perhaps some other time. The acts to which they're admitting are so appalling, I would prefer to put them out of my mind for a very long time."

"Of course, my dear, I certainly don't want to upset you further. When we get back to the cottage, I'll take a look to see what Jacob and Henry are doing. I'll then keep them occupied while you look in from the outside so that you can see how well your son is growing. If they're playing outside, I'll take them inside the cottage so that neither of them will see you. What do you think? Will that make you happy or sad?

"However I feel Marion, I do so wish to see Henry and shall do as you suggest. Thank you very much indeed."

Margory brushed away an escaping tear and embraced her very good friend.

Chapter 71

Solicitous as ever, Ruth turned to her mistress:

"Oh Mistress Margory, it grieves me to see you so sad. I do hope you don't mind my suggesting that you rest the moment we are back at The Manor. The ride has been a long one and distressing for you, I think, in many ways. Although I know not the reason for our visit to Chelmsford – and I do not wish to know unless it would help you to tell me – it has clearly made you unhappy. And for that I'm very sorry."

"Yes, you are right, Ruth, that is a kind thought and a sensible one. I shall speak to Goodwife Sykes on our return to hear what, if anything of import, has taken place in my absence. I shall then take to my bed for I do, indeed, feel very tired and sorrowful. Here we are now."

Glancing around in case she saw the stable hand who she now thought may be watching her at Arthur's command, there was no sign of him. Instead, her trusted servant, Goodwife Sykes, was walking slowly towards the horses. Yes, Arthur was right in saying that she was getting old. However, that was all the more reason for Margory to ensure that she was safe and cared for. While Arthur was speaking increasingly about dismissing some of the servants, she would make her own plans for keeping them. She was sorry that she hadn't been able to visit her friend, Bess, at either Chatsworth or Hardwick Hall, particularly as her husband, Sir William St Loe, had died the previous year. Mary, Bess's youngest child, was ten years old, so it would be very pleasant to try to see her, as well as any of the other five children. Bess would be happy, she felt sure, to advise her on what she should do about her ageing servant as well as some of her other concerns. But mainly, it would just be so nice to see Bess as she was such an interesting person.

"How pleased I am to see your safe return, Mistress. Master Arthur has not yet returned and all is well here. I hope that your journey was satisfactory."

"As much as it could have been, Goodwife Sykes. But I am now very tired and I am sure that Ruth would like to rest, too. I shall go to my bed for a while. Would you ask cook to prepare something light for me to enjoy later."

"Yes, of course, Mistress. I shall await your presence after you have rested."

Chapter 72

"Come Beth, let us go to the inn to drink some smoke. Of course, I know that you would like to do the same, while drinking sweet Spanish wine. I've heard of an excellent inn, the Three Fishes, which I'm told, some of the staff of Sir Gilbert Gerard, the Queen's Attorney General, may frequent. His is a very old, prestigious family that have lived in this area for generations and own many acres of land. I intend to make myself known in these parts as someone to be respected. I am gathering a great sum of money that will enable me to build a house as fine as Chatsworth. Well, perhaps not quite so fine, but fine enough. You would be very fortunate to be its mistress." Arthur glanced fleetingly at Beth and winked at her look of surprise.

"But sir, you are already wed to another…" Beth drew away from Arthur a little and frowned. "And please forgive my asking, but when you say that you are gathering a great sum of money, how will you be doing that?"

"Don't you worry your pretty head, my love. My wife lives many miles from here and has no idea where I am, ever. As for my raising money, management of the home and looking after children is what women should do. Anything to do with finances should be left to the man of the house. So let's not speak of it again. Oh, here is the inn. Although I'm not a man of God, I know that this area is a place of pilgrimage for those who come to All Hallows' church; this is where they rest and take refreshment."

Beth still looked unsure, so Arthur led her to a quiet area.

"But sir, these patrons do not all look to be wealthy, although some certainly are. I feel a little uncomfortable in such a place."

"You're still anxious, my dear, with no cause at all. Remember that when I am by your side, you are perfectly safe. Now, to clear your brow, I shall ask for a large white wine for you. Oh and see who is entering the establishment – a member of the clergy, no less. Now do you feel in better spirits? Perhaps you didn't know that the last Abbot of Whalley is said to have named the inn, not only due to the convergence of the three rivers, but because of the biblical significance of the three fishes. Indeed, you and I shall come here again as I feel an affinity with an inn that represents growth from lowly beginnings. I, myself, began with only three fishes and look at me now! Lord of the Manor in Hertfordshire and about to provide you, my beauty, with another manor house in this area."

"And how do you intend to do that, sir?"

Beth's brow continued to look troubled so Arthur turned to face her. Touching her cheek, he said,

"Too many questions, dear Beth. Too many questions. If you continue to question me in this way, I shall become displeased. You wouldn't want that, now, would you? Perhaps you should return to Hertfordshire as I would like to know who my wife meets in my absence. I care not for my son's abduction as I am able to create another heir easily."

"Are you proposing, sir, that I should spy on the lady of the house? I'm not sure…"

"If you're not sure, Beth, perhaps you would prefer me to tell my wife that you agreed to accompany me to Lancashire? I'm sure you realise that your midwifery skills would no longer be required by our tenants or, in future, by my wife, should your tongue turn to such impertinence. That's better. I see that your common sense has prevailed. I now wish to speak to the landlord so I suggest that you remain seated here quietly with your wine until I say I am ready to leave. I think you should consider our conversation because it may be time for you to hire a horse for your return to Hertfordshire."

"But sir. You're not proposing that I make that journey alone, are you?"

"What I am proposing is that you do as I wish and continue to stay here with me or, if that is not to your liking, that you leave. It is your choice. Now please don't delay me in speaking to the landlord as I have important work to do in these parts. And don't cry like that or the other customers will think that I'm mistreating you."

Chapter 73

"Ah, innkeeper, my good man. I would like to learn the magnificent game of chess. Are we about to leave this board game to the ladies? I understand that Mary, Queen of Scots as well as our own Elizabeth play the game well, although, sad to say, Queen Mary was not so fortunate. Please let me know which of your patrons I should speak to. Why are you looking at me in that way? I trust that my clothes befit your fine inn. If not, I shall go elsewhere. I'll have you know that, in Hertfordshire, I am Lord of the Manor and intend to buy another large house in this area, too. Perhaps I should buy ale somewhere else. What do you think?"

"Do you have an income of more than £100, sir? As you know, our late King Henry is said to have forbidden any member of the gentry with less than that figure to play any game for money. Why do you hesitate?"

"Er…I hesitate because, of course, my income is much in excess of that although you are quite correct in assuming me to be a member of the gentry. Also, as I am not inclined to archery, I shall continue to play dice in addition to learning the art of chess. I repeat, shall I do that elsewhere or here? Are you able to afford to lose customers, my man? I intend to have increasing influence in this area. In fact, in view of your attitude, I shall enjoy my games at several establishments, particularly other inns."

Chapter 74

"Goodwife Sykes, wonderful news! My friend, Bess, has married once more, this time to the Earl of Shrewsbury, and has become Countess. I am invited to visit her as soon as I can arrange it while the weather is fine. As Arthur is away and, once more, I know not when he will return, I shall ask Marion and Abner if Hugh can look after the estate as he knows it so well. I really don't want to refuse this wonderful invitation but cannot leave The Manor unattended. Please ask Lucy to come to see me as I shall leave her to run the household with your good self and the other servants.

The Countess tells me that, although she and her husband are well known at court, the wedding was a quiet affair and that I am not to spend money that I do not have on either special clothing for the visit or a present. That is very thoughtful as I have money for neither. However, I shall consider giving her a linen handkerchief with a pretty, lace edging which my dear mother left me.

I was particularly delighted that Bess and Sir William who, you will remember, was Bess's second husband, were able to come to my wedding to Arthur as Sir William so sadly died later that year. They supported my dear, late father in spite of the fact that Bess is Protestant. Mary was still on the throne, of course, and we enjoyed a Catholic wedding as I did not wish to be disrespectful to my faith or my parents and grandparents who had practised it. Even our Protestant Queen Elizabeth is a great diplomat in accepting the best of both faiths, when that is possible. She doesn't tread an easy balance, but she succeeds. Although I hope not to blaspheme when I say this but, were it not for the fact that I am a devout Roman Catholic, I know that I would like to get to know Her Majesty better. She does, after all, enjoy the music of William Byrd and Thomas Tallis, both of whom are of the Catholic persuasion. Also, it is spoken that her Attorney General, Sir Gilbert Gerard, is Protestant at court yet a Papist in his own, vast lands in the North West. I shall need to reply to my friend, Bess, to say that I am very much looking forward to enjoying her company again as it is some time since I have had the pleasure of speaking to her. The invitation is, of course, for both me and my husband. However, I know neither where he is nor when he will be returning. I would like to say that I am disappointed about that but I am not. Arthur seems to be reverting to his previous behaviour of staying away for quite some time without informing me when he will return, if that is his intention. So I shall take three of the bravest stable hands to accompany me and our best horses. As Arthur took our only coach, I shall either hire one or ask my dear friend, Marion, if I may borrow one of theirs. There has been such a good harvest again this year that many will be occupied and the roads will be clearer. Should my husband return in my absence, please address his needs attentively and inform him of my whereabouts, then rest when he leaves. I am so looking forward to seeing Bess and visiting Chatsworth again."

With that, Margory embraced her faithful servant and went to the library to write a note to Hugh.

Chapter 75

"My dear Margory, welcome to Chatsworth. How well you look, but you must be tired following your long journey. Do I detect a little sadness, too? Your bedchamber has been prepared so do rest for as long as you need. I have told cook that I shall let her know when you are refreshed and ready to have a meal."

"You are kind and astute as always, Bess. I am truly looking forward to speaking to you about several matters, as I have experienced your wisdom in the past. And yes, the journey has taken several days so thank you for suggesting that I rest. I'm also looking forward to hearing about your wedding to the Earl."

***

"You look so much better now, dear. Let us retire to one of the smaller living rooms so that you can tell me all about your activities, good and not so good. I want to hear everything."

Margory felt her whole being, from shoulders to feet, begin to relax for the first time in a long while as she proceeded to tell her friend what had been happening.

"How kind you are, Bess, and thank you so much for inviting me to your beautiful home. I was delighted to know that you have married again. You have had such a sad time with your previous three husbands dying – first, Robert Barlow, then Sir William Cavendish and, latterly, Sir William St Loe. I shall pray that your marriage to the 6th Earl of Shrewsbury will be a long and happy one."

"Thank you, my dear. I'm fortunate that six of my eight children survive. But let me see, I know that you have a son.

How old is he now? I'm sure he gives you a great deal of pleasure."

"Bess, I cannot begin to describe the depth of my love for Henry, who is now two. I'm sure all mothers say this, but I do think that he is very advanced for his age. He is, in fact, one of the reasons I wish to speak to you. Although he is a beautiful, clever baby, Arthur treats him very badly."

Margory hesitated. In spite of the dreadful way Arthur had treated Henry and herself, she found it difficult to be disloyal. She had, after all, chosen to walk down the aisle with Arthur, several years ago. It had been her choice. Indeed, in spite of his reluctance, she had persuaded him to marry her. This was all her fault. But the good part was Henry. She adored him, and he was worth everything she was going through. What she would not tolerate, however, was Arthur's treatment of her beloved boy. Yes, she would tell Bess all about that. Bess would know what to do. At the same time, she would mention how helpful Hugh had always been.

Bess turned so that she was giving Margory all her attention, a look of shock on her face. She listened without speaking. However, when Margory proceeded to describe how badly Arthur had beaten Henry and could contain her tears no longer, Bess said,

"I cannot believe what I am hearing, Margory. Why would a grown man and father treat his child in this way?"

"He does so, Bess, in order to hurt me and to show that he is master of the house. But when Henry could barely crawl following the last beating, my very good friend, Marion, took him and takes care of him. Not only does Arthur not know where Henry is, he cares not either. As Henry was conceived forcibly, my husband knows that he can create another heir in the same way, any time he wishes.

All he cares about is becoming richer and having an heir to follow him."

"My dear girl, this is terrible news. Where is your husband now?"

"I know not. At the time of our marriage and my parents' death, he left and bought a home elsewhere in the country - I believe it to have been somewhere in the North West of England - with one of my parents' servants. She bore him two children but has recently returned to tell me how this happened. He was gone for four years. He has now left The Manor again accompanied, I assume, by another young woman. But I know Arthur well. Whatever money he gains, by gambling, he will lose and, when he has no more to spend, he will return, claiming his place as Lord of the Manor yet again."

"This is indeed a dreadful dilemma, Margory. Knowing you as I do, and unlike many who would behave differently, as your Catholic faith does not allow you to divorce, there is no obvious solution. Nor, of course, do you fall into any of the four reasons to dissolve the marriage. But I shall think about it. I believe you have done exactly the right thing in ensuring that Henry is shielded from harm. Clearly, your friend, Marion, is a very good friend indeed. One day, surely, you can be reunited fully with your son. Whether your friendship with Hugh can deepen is unknown to anyone, of course, at the moment. Personally, I am happy to hear that you have his support, even though he may not know everything about your circumstances with Arthur.

Now, I shall ask one of the servants to light more fires as I'm sure, like me, you are beginning to feel much colder. But do continue, as I feel you have even more to tell me."

Little by little, Margory told about her meeting with Agnes Waterhouse, including her having seen Sir Gilbert Gerard.

"Oh yes, I've met Gilbert. What a politician he is. But then, our dear queen does surround herself with clever people, being highly intelligent herself. I have recently spent quite some time at court so was able to see for myself how the queen conducts her affairs. Believe me, she does an excellent job. Not that she's a spendthrift like her father, far from it, but because she is very careful to follow the religious route of her people. And speaking of religion, I may be sending you a message in connection with Mary of the Scots. You will be sorry to hear, I know, that rumour has it she recently lost a babe while at Loch Leven Castle."

Margory gasped, knowing, from her own experience, what a traumatic time that would have been for Mary.

"I am so very sorry to hear that, Bess, and I do hope that she received the best of care."

"We can only hope so. However, there have been so many difficult events in Scotland for Queen Mary that it is said she intends to come South. Should that happen, I am sure our Queen Elizabeth will ensure that she remains in the North of the country. She is, after all, Catholic, and our own Queen will want to steer her English ship away from potential trouble. However, that is a little in the future. I mention it partly because, as you are of the same religion, you may find it interesting to meet Queen Mary, should that be possible, once she has taken up residence South of the border. That is all I shall say for now. However, once again, I know that you will exercise a high level of discretion, if you are invited to meet her. Once it is known what further plans our Queen has for Mary, I shall know whether and how my family and I shall be involved."

"Of course."

Margory listened as, being the daughter of a Lord of the Manor, she had often sat on the fringes of important people. Thinking back for a moment, she felt a little sad that her ambitious mother had never achieved the level she wished in society – although she had tried hard to do so.

Now, although she, herself, had never been interested in climbing the social ladder, Margory felt extremely privileged to have been taken into the countess's confidence. What she had said was very interesting and Margory was looking forward to thinking about it further. Although her father had become involved in politics, it had never been a subject that had interested her, in spite of the fact that she spoke three languages (although she knew that Queen Elizabeth spoke at least five fluently). The only time Margory had become interested in education, really, was when she had been asked, by her wonderful father, to teach Arthur reading, writing and arithmetic. And what a bad decision that had turned out to be. She hoped she had matured considerably since those days.

"Margory. Margory. Are you all right, my dear? You looked to be far away in your thoughts. You had finished telling me about Agnes Waterhouse, I think. What I can do, if you agree, is to advise Sir Gilbert about your husband's gambling. From what you say, it sounds as though he will stop at nothing to enter the world of the wealthy. Sir Gilbert will want to ensure that his gambling remains legitimate, particularly as a number of his servants play. Just leave that with me, my dear.

Chapter 76

"No, innkeeper, my lady friend has returned to Hertfordshire on a hired horse. The game of dice is very enjoyable but even fine inns such as the Olde Man & Scythe are not appropriate places for such as she."

"So are you playing dice at several inns or do you frequent taverns and ale houses, too?"

"Certainly not. Someone in my position plays only in the best of inns. Last week the Seven Stars in Manchester was fortunate to gain by my patronage and next week I intend to play at the Castle Inn in Hornby. It is my intention to stay here for some time. I wish to get to know the area and those of importance in it." His chest puffed with pride.

"As Lord of the Manor in Greenwillows, Hertfordshire, I employ many staff. And, of course, my wife manages the household, like her mother before her. So the manor is looked after at all times and does not require my constant presence."

"Oh and who was your wife's mother, may I ask, sir?"

"You may as well know that my wife's parents were recusants and put to the stake, quite rightly, in my opinion. Although, of course, I keep that thought to myself so as not to upset my wife. Although her father frequented the wrong church, he did well by me and I liked him. I care not who visits which church as I rarely visit any, although I wish that to remain between you and me, too."

"Recusants, you say. Better not to spread that word in this area, what with the Scottish queen expected and all. Bad enough that Queen Elizabeth's Attorney General appears to do her bidding when at court but turns papist on returning to his vast lands here in the North West."

Ignoring this, Arthur was very interested to hear that Queen Mary was expected.

"Where will the Scottish queen be staying?"

"I understand that she will be put in the charge of Sir Francis Knollys who, it is thought, will become Treasurer of the Chamber."

If Arthur's ears could have twitched, they would have done so at that news. He knew that Treasurer of the Chamber meant that Sir Francis would have considerable financial responsibilities. Yes, he would look into that further. It had been many years since he had knocked on the main door of The Manor in Greenwillows. Much had happened since then and, now, he would have no hesitation whatsoever in approaching Sir Francis. Indeed, he may demand an audience with the Queen Mary herself. Arthur straightened. He could smell success around the corner. But the innkeeper was still speaking.

"So your wife inherited the family manor and land, did she? Was that before or after you were married?"

"That's a disrespectful question and I'll mind you to keep your curiosity to yourself. Yes, I seem to recall playing dice with some of his Lordship's men recently. As I say, I care not which church they inhabit provided they can play a sporting game."

"Quite. Well, I can't stand around gossiping. There's always work to be done here."

Chapter 77

"Have you played dice with this man from Hertfordshire who claims to be Lord of the Manor there? Only got his word for that, of course. Why is he here? Be careful. Although I haven't played a game with him, I've been told by several men that he plays with weighted dice. That's in spite of the fact that he's seen in possession of ivory dice. Holds and shows true dice in his right hand, then exchanges those for false dice in his left. I've heard it said that this man, Arthur by name, I think, insists on playing on a board marked with diagonal lines. After the stake has been laid in the pool and dice rolled as many times as each wishes, others are so busy adding up their own scores that they don't notice that this man's dice falls closest to 31 every time. I'm told he doesn't stay long enough for this to be realised but moves on to the next drinking house. However, this has happened so many times now that he is close to a number of men reporting him. He's starting to be so cocky that our friend, John Allard, who, as we all know, isn't the cleverest of men, has been defrauded of six shillings and five pence."

"What? John's a good friend of mine and certainly cannot afford to lose that sort of money. I shall not only watch out for this man called Arthur but shall spread the word at local drinking places. Thanks, George."

"Yes, I intend to do the same."

"Her Majesty's Attorney General would not be best pleased were he to hear that his staff are losing money in this way. Although, of course, Sir Gilbert spends more time at court than on his lands hereabout, so is unlikely to hear. He's only just returned, I understand, from Essex where he attended the first execution for witchcraft. Although his return to his lands here was delayed by his going back to court to inform Her Majesty about the trial as well as hearing the latest music by her favourite composers. I wouldn't want to be this man, Arthur, if Sir Gilbert does find out."

Chapter 78

"Get him! That's the man who cheated in our game of dice. I know Sir Gilbert will not tolerate cheats, nor his servants losing hard-earned money."

But they were too late. Arthur had had his coach prepared and ready should it be found out how he was earning his money.

"Fast as you can. The weather's taking a turn for the worse."

Chapter 79

"Oh, your Lordship, do come in from the freezing cold. I have ensured that all the fires are lit, should you or her Ladyship return."

In spite of the pain in her knees, Goodwife Sykes dipped a deep curtsey and lowered her eyes.

"Get out of my way, you old dolt. What do you mean, '...should...her Ladyship return.' Where is my wife and why isn't she here to greet me? More importantly, what is HE doing here? Are you telling me that you are in charge of the household and he has moved in. I don't believe this. I go away for a few days – er, well, that was my original intention. Perhaps it has been more than a few days – and when I return, my wife is nowhere to be seen and her beloved who claims not to have shared her bed, is living in my home."

"Don't you dare..."

"Oh I dare! Get out! I dare because I am the lord of this manor and I have returned. I believe I have warned you before. Don't ever let me find you on my land again. If I do, I shall not be responsible for my actions. For your information, I always carry a pistol. As my wife will inform you, I used it successfully when we journeyed into London several years ago. I shall not hesitate to use it again on you or anyone else who comes on to my land uninvited. Do I make myself clear?"

"Your wife..."

"Ah, you admit that she is my wife, do you. Where is she? Still abed where you left her, no doubt."

"As you have returned, my services are clearly no longer required and I shall be on my way. I don't intend to be insulted further. Goodwife Sykes. Thank you for your hospitality. It will not be forgotten."

"Whatever those services were, you have just uttered the most sensible words yet. Be gone. Now. My wife has a great deal of explaining to do – wherever she is."

Grabbing Goodwife Sykes's sleeve, he began to drag her inside.

"Leave Goodwife Sykes be. She's no longer young…"

"Are you still here? No, and soon she will no longer be employed by me either."

Hugh embraced Goodwife Sykes whose eyes filled with tears.

"Thank you for your kindness, sir. I shall tell her Ladyship what happened."

"You will tell her Ladyship whatever I allow you to tell her. Get inside and get on with your duties before I put you out on to the street now, with only the clothes you stand in."

"Would you like me to stay, Goodwife Sykes?"

"No, sir. No good can come from your presence so it will be better for you to leave."

"Do as the woman bids. Leave now and stay away."

Turning to Goodwife Sykes.

"I ask again. Where is my wife? I do declare that the moment my back is turned she leaves behind her wifely duties. Well, wherever she is, she will be punished on her return."

Chapter 80

"My dear girl, you can't leave in this severely cold weather. You must spend Christmas with us. Ours is such a large family, what with my six beloved children and the Earl's six, you won't have time to be unhappy."

"That is most kind, Bess. I do wish that I knew where my husband is, but I don't. So I shall send a message to The Manor, telling him where I am. It may be that he would like to join me. Would that be convenient to you, if he so wishes?"

"Of course, Margory. Whatever I think of Arthur, he is your husband and if he wishes to join you here, that will be entirely satisfactory."

Margory remained silent. She knew that, should Arthur decide to join her at Chatsworth it would be because of the wealth of its owners not in order to be in her company. Looking down at her lap, she smoothed her dress in disappointment.

"You are too kind, Bess. I shall ask one of my servants to take a note to The Manor, although I know not whether he has returned there."

"Margory. As he left without informing you of his destination nor how long he would be away, that is all you can do. Many would not even do that, having been treated in the way he has treated, not only you, but your dear child, too."

"Oh dear, were it not for this severe weather, I would return myself as I miss little Henry so very much. I'm concerned that he may forget me. He's so very young, after all."

"I wouldn't hear of you travelling at the moment, Margory. You must remember that Henry is in the safe and kind care of your good friend. As soon as the weather improves, you can return, knowing that you will not be taking risks. I know you realise that, as a mother, you must stay safe for your son's sake."

"Your words are wise, as always, Bess, and I shall do as you suggest. You're quite right in saying that I know Henry is safe and well cared for. In the meantime, I thank you for inviting me to share your Christmas. I'm only sorry that I cannot give presents. However, I shall help to decorate your beautiful home."

"Oh that isn't all you can do to help, Margory dear! Our tenants and servants will be joining us for the day after Boxing Day as they are given that day off to take presents to their families. Also, for those who cannot walk very well, I shall be visiting them in their homes. My children, of course, are old enough to help, ranging as they are in age from 19 to 11. It would be most helpful if you could also help with all these preparations."

"I would like that very much, particularly as that is what I used to do with my mother at this time of year."

"That's settled then."

"There is something else I have been intending to mention, too, my dear."

Margory drew closer as Bess lowered her voice, and looked at her friend, expectantly.

"I do know, of course, that, like our Queen of Scots, you are of the Roman persuasion and I do not intend to prevent you from worshipping in your usual way at this important time of year. However, I would ask that you do so discreetly…"

"Thank…"

"Allow me to finish, Margory. I feel happy to allow this as our own, dear Queen Elizabeth does the same on more than one occasion when, for example, she is enjoying the music of both Byrd and Tallis. You may know that they worship as you do. What our queen has instructed is that they do not do this openly. However, she has, in spite of that, granted an exclusive licence to print and publish music which gives them a 21-year monopoly. I ask the same of you. Please be very careful not to worship openly."

"Dear Bess. Thank you so much. I shall ensure that I worship privately while I am your guest. Indeed, I do so usually anyway, at The Manor, as we have a private chapel. However, no-one knows that and I do know that you will not tell others either. I do thank you from the bottom of my heart as this is so important to me. As you say, particularly at this time of year."

Bess embraced Margory and gave her a light kiss on the cheek.

Chapter 81

"Master Arthur, a messenger has just delivered a note for you."

"Begone, woman, and bring Lucy to me. This is probably another ransom request so yet another I shall ignore. What good is a child who doesn't live at home. None whatsoever. I shall simply make another to be my heir when my wife deigns to return. In the meantime, Sykes, as I said, bring Lucy to me. What does this note say? Oh, it's from my dear wife, inviting me to join her at Chatsworth. How fortunate that she taught me to read all those years ago. Although I would very much like to be part of such wealth, Chatsworth is much too near the inns I have been frequenting and word may well have reached Chatsworth's servants.

"Are you still here, Sykes! I thought I told you to bring Lucy to me – now! Not tomorrow. I really must get rid of you and surround myself by pretty young servants who do my bidding – and quickly. Ah, there you are, Lucy. What kept you? I wish to ride over my land to see that it is in good order and you will accompany me. Yes, change into your riding clothes and don't take all day about it."

"I have just learned that my wife is staying at Chatsworth with the Countess of Shrewsbury. I would have joined her but I want to make sure that my land is being taken care of. Also, the weather is not good for long rides and I don't wish to take the carriage on this occasion. I shall not leave The Manor until the weather improves. In the meantime, I assume that you are in charge of the household management, Lucy, just as you were at our home in Lancashire. You do remember how to manage the household of a great house, I assume don't you. If not, I shall need to invite another lady friend to join me here. Is that clear?"

"Yes, Master Arthur, I do recall. When her Ladyship left she asked me to take charge of the household until her return. Although I hadn't done such management for several years. I know the staff well, of course, and have been happy to work with them."

"Don't you forget that, for the moment, you are the lady of the house so becoming too friendly with the servants would not be appropriate. You will not be working with them, you will be commanding them. Look at me when I'm speaking to you. Do you understand? I shall be dispensing with the services of servants who are old and can no longer keep up with the fast pace of a manor house such as this. So for you to develop friendships with them would not be fitting. Am I making myself clear? If my wife is going to start leaving our land whenever she pleases, I shall need to ensure that I know about it and can put my own friends in charge if I am also absent. What I do not intend to happen is for my wife's friends to organise The Manor. What would people think? Not only would my own servants gossip but they would spread the word throughout the county. Before long, thieves and vagabonds would learn that neither the Master nor Mistress are at home and who knows what would happen."

"But sir, my Lady left Master Hugh…"

"Master Hugh, Master Hugh. If his name should pass your lips one more time, you will be put out on to the road where I found you all those years ago. You ungrateful wench. Have you forgotten already how I rescued you and took you to be mistress of a grand house, just as grand as The Manor? I can see that I shall have to start treating you like the servant you were when I rescued you. Who would come to your rescue then? No-one. Because you have no family other than my two children you bore."

"But they are my…"

"Are you contradicting me yet again, Lucy."

"Don't drag me like that, sir."

"I shall drag you how I like and put you where I like. These cellars are dark and rat-infested. See how you like spending a few days down there without food and water."

"No, sir. Please, sir. Don't do this to me, the mother of your children. I beg you. I'm afraid of the dark."

"You should have thought of that when you were speaking contrary to my wishes, then. All right, because I'm a kind, generous member of the gentry, I shall only leave you in the dark, damp cellar for one day."

"Excuse me, sir, you didn't hear my knocking. Is Lucy all right? Why is she crying so? In the cellar. You can't put her in the cellar with the rats, sir. She will go out of her mind. Aaaah!"

"Sir, you hit Goodwife Sykes so hard she has your red fingerprints on her cheek. Please don't hit her again. I'll happily go into the cellar provided you don't touch her again."

"Oh you would, would you. Well, let me tell you this. If the two of you don't start to obey my orders, I shall throw both of you into the cellar and leave you there to rot. Do you understand? Remember who is master of The Manor and who is not. Remember that my wife left our estate unattended and asked a friend of hers to tend it in my absence. I am the Lord of the Manor, not Hugh Taylor or whatever his name is. If I find him on my land once more, he will join the two of you in the cellar. If you want to gossip about something, spread that word so that it will reach him in Brockminster. I shall not tolerate interference in my life and my land and I shall do whatever it takes to ensure that my land remains in my own safe hands, whether I am here or not."

"How will you…?"

"Do my ears deceive me or are you questioning my word yet again. Get back to the kitchens where you both belong. I don't wish to see either of your faces until I command it."

Chapter 82

"Henry and Charles, would you help Mistress Margory with the holly, ivy, laurel and yew. William, I shall need your help with the mistletoe and box. You know how the servants wish for a swift kiss. Usually, I would ask the servants to decorate, but if we all do it, I hope it will take your mind off the fact that little Henry isn't with us, Margory. Frances: Did you know that one of King Henry's favourite carols was The Holly and The Ivy? Have you chosen the carols we shall sing?"

"I like 'Nowell Nowell'."

Not to be out-done, William countered, "'Good King Wenceslaus' – it's much livelier!"

"We shall start with those this evening, when the dancing begins. Also, don't forget to ask Mistress Margory which is her favourite carol."

"Oh, I enjoy so many carols that I shall leave the choice to your lovely children. What I shall particularly delight in is the dancing. It's so long since I danced that I shall take pleasure in doing it to whatever is chosen. And thank you, Bess, for thinking of Henry."

Eventually, the great chamber at Chatsworth looked so splendid that Bess suggested the children left her and Margory to their light supper.

"Frances. Please make sure that Cook is ready to prepare goose, pork, coneys, capon, mutton, chicken and beef. That's a long list for you to remember! I may also speak to her about woodcock and turkey." Turning to Margory, she asked, "I'm sure you know, my dear, that our good King Henry began to have turkey served at Christmas. Have you managed to serve it at The Manor yet?"

"No, but I shall be happy to enjoy it with you before suggesting we include it at The Manor. I know that Arthur will be delighted to try something new, particularly when recommended by yourself and our late king."

And so, Margory and Bess sat by the crackling fire, with the smell of the burning beeswax candles, and rested their weary bones.

"In spite of our feeling very tired, this is so very pleasant, Bess. Thank you for inviting me into your home at this wonderful time of year."

A knock preceded one of the butlers.

"Countess. You have visitors who tell me they were invited. Shall I show them in?"

"Yes, of course, Ralph, in a few moments. Thank you."

"Margory, dear, I have a surprise for you. Let me look at you. Yes, you look perfectly lovely."

"Why, Bess. I'm so sorry to be disturbing you as you have invited your friends. Oh…" Margory gasped as, first Marion came into the room, holding Henry's hand as he tottered in, followed by Abner and Jacob. Then in walked Hugh." Margory's eyes filled with tears.

"Oh, Bess, Bess. This is the very best Christmas present you could have given me."

Henry then ran into Margory's arms and she could hold back the flood gates no longer. Once again, just like what seemed a very long time ago, his finger prodded a fat tear as it rolled down his mother's face.

"Why mama crying? Are you sad?"

"Mama is crying because she is very, very happy, my dear little man." Margory said, hugging him to her as he lay his head on her shoulder.

"Oh Bess, Marion, Abner. Thank you. But how did you make this journey as the weather is so severe."

"Lord Winchester told us we must use his largest coach and best horses. You know yourself what a very kind person he is, Margory. He also insisted that Hugh accompanied us as Lord Winchester now has a second, very capable Deputy Estate Manager."

"Indeed, I do know his kindness and, when we return, I must visit him to thank him in person. One day, Bess, I would like to introduce you to his Lordship whose generosity almost equals your own."

"I look forward to that, Margory. And I'm delighted that the three of you could join us with Henry."

Marion glanced at Margory as she replied.

"Yes, we were so pleased that Hugh was able to help us make this difficult journey. With your permission, Countess, perhaps Margory could be spared to show Hugh part of your glorious estate. I believe you have almost 2,000 acres here – is that right?"

"Yes, you're quite right, Marion. I'm sure Master Hugh would like to take a walk before retiring. There will be plenty of time for further exploration during your stay at Chatsworth."

As always, Bess showed great perception and, without glancing at Margory, said,

"That would be most helpful. I shall ask my head housekeeper to show you to your rooms."

At that, little Henry clung even tighter to his mother.

"That's all right, darling. You are going to stay with me."

Chapter 83

"I haven't had such a wonderful Christmas as this for a very long time, Bess. I thank you from the bottom of my heart. Christmas is a time for family and friends and, here, I am surrounded by both. At a time when love is acknowledged to be the best thing in the world, I am immersed, at every turn, in that love. Not only do I thank you, but I thank the good Lord who has made this possible. I shall never forget this."

"Mama. What is this?" Henry pointed at the sausage-shaped item that had just been placed on the table.

"That's Christmas pudding, darling, and very delicious it is, too. It has meat, oatmeal and spices in it so I shall give you a small portion to start with. If my friend, Bess, agrees, you may even be allowed a little more. However, there are people who are less fortunate than we are, so some of this delicious food will be saved to give to them."

Henry looked at his mother so adoringly she thought her melting heart would be seen by everyone.

Chapter 84

"Can I come, too, mama?"

"Darling, it is extremely cold at the moment and beginning to snow. Did you hear Aunt Marion saying that the Thames has frozen over. Master Hugh and I shall be doing a lot of walking and I don't want to tire you out before our busy day tomorrow."

"Please, mama. Perhaps you won't come back…"

He was clinging to her leg so tightly, Margory couldn't move anyway. Lifting him up, she gazed into his little face with its trembling lip and thought she would never be able to lose sight of him again – ever. However, her memory of Arthur's beating coincided with a gentle touch on her arm. Turning, she saw Marion looking at this scene of love and knew that she understood.

"Come, Jacob. Take Henry's hand and we'll go to the kitchen."

Henry was clearly unsure about this different turn of events, knowing and trusting Marion, the woman he called 'aunt' and Jacob, his good friend. Reluctantly, he succumbed to Margory's gently giving him to Marion who set him down and put his little hand into Jacob's bigger one.

"Come on, Henry, let's see what cook has for us."

Although this scene broke Margory's heart as she had never denied Henry anything and was loathe to do so now, the conversation she would be having with Hugh, she knew, may occasionally verge on the personal and would be inappropriate for Henry to hear. He rarely missed anything, after all.

So, giving Henry a kiss, and telling him she wouldn't be long, Margory and Hugh started their walk, with Margory ensuring that there was a certain distance between them. Anyone observing them would easily have thought they had only just met. For both, it was a test of their strength that they ensured neither touched the other.

"Look at all these beautiful ponds and fountains turned to ice," Hugh commented, "They're almost as beautiful as you, my dear and, like you, need to be protected."

"Thank you, Hugh, but please do not resort to personal comments. Not only am I a married woman, but Arthur and I have a 2-year-old child, as you know."

"Yes, clearly, you and Arthur made love…"

This quick change of conversation to the very personal surprised Margory somewhat. She pulled her warm cape closer, in an effort to gain comfort.

"Made love is not quite accurate, Hugh. But let us not talk of it, please. I think there are some seats within the West garden wall. Let us find them."

But Margory's change of subject was not to deter Hugh.

"I simply want to know, Margory, that you are happy. If you assure me that you are, I shall refrain from pursuing a personal path."

"My son makes me very happy indeed, Hugh, and that is all I am prepared to say."

Hugh had seen that determined set of Margory's mouth before and, as though echoing her mood, it began to snow so hard that the two had to quickly return to the house. Scooping up her gown, Margory turned back, almost slipping as she avoided Hugh's helping hand.

For once, Margory was pleased to see the snow falling between her walk with Hugh and their conversation as her mood was beginning to cool. It was all too easy for her to recall the walk she had taken with Arthur when their time in the woods had become intimate. Just in time, Arthur's mother had intervened. But that had been Margory's chance to insist that her relationship with Arthur was put on the formal footing of marriage. Yes, she only ever had herself to blame for taking the lead in their walk down the aisle. However, that was in the past. All she could do now was to learn from her mistakes going forwards. How selfish youth could be. Now she was paying the price.

Chapter 85

Reader. Have you ever experienced a near-perfect Christmas? For me, it is absolutely perfect when surrounded by loving family and caring friends. Although I could have wished for a loving husband to share it with me, few experiences are totally perfect, are they? Instead, I had a beautiful son and loyal friends. Far more than many. And all enjoyed in the fine surroundings of a magnificent house and beautiful grounds. I had much to thank the Lord for and, once my dear Henry was fast asleep, I dropped to my knees and expressed my appreciation to the God who had delivered me safely into the hands of those around me. Was it a perfect prayer? I think not, as my thoughts, on that night, did not travel South to The Manor, other than to hope that Goodwife Sykes and my other servants were well. After all, I knew not where my husband was resting his head that night. And I feel guilty when saying that neither did I care. Arthur always did what Arthur wished and cared not who he may be hurting in the process. No, you see, reader, I am not perfect. But, for the moment, I was very, very happy. It was not to last.

Chapter 86

"Thank you for your kind offer, Marion, but I cannot risk Arthur seeing all of us together when I return. And that's in spite of the fact that I know not whether he will be at The Manor. The servants and I left together and we shall return together. Also, it will mean that none of my faithful servants at The Manor will need to avoid the truth, should they see you, Henry, Abner and, in particular, Hugh, return with me. Although I am becoming used to Arthur's beating of me, I simply cannot and shall not risk his repeated beating of Henry, should he catch a glimpse of him. No, we came alone and we shall return alone. But I do thank you most sincerely, my dear friend, for suggesting that we all return together. The day is bright and, should the weather remain clear, it will not be a long journey."

After embracing her good friend, Bess, Margory and her servants left Chatsworth, with Henry's calling for her ringing in her ears. Were it not for the fact of Arthur's cruel beating of Henry, she could not have borne to leave him behind yet again. She would need to pray even harder on her return to The Manor for guidance on what she should do as she just could not continue to distress Henry in this way.

Chapter 87

"Ah, there you are, my dear. I thought you had forgotten that we shall be returning to the North West today. Lucy: I am leaving you in charge of the household's organisation which I believe you have undertaken before, as I know not when my wife will deign to return from her wealthy friend's hospitality. Also, I have put Thomas in charge of the estate and, if he carries out those duties well, I shall promote him to estate manager. In that way, it will be entirely unnecessary for my wife to arrange for her own friend to take over my estate. She seems to forget that I am Lord of The Manor. But then, her memory is not what it was and I still need to do something about that. How could a mother lose her child? Were it not so serious, it would be a cause for mirth. But my heir shall be replaced when my wife and I take to our bed. At the moment, of course, I know not when that will be as I am looking forward to continuing my gambling in the North West of the country. I have never met so many dolts who clearly do not realise that, however well they play, I play better. I shall, nevertheless, visit several inns, rather than just one. In that way, my method of play will not be understood until I have left for the next inn. Although I shall make it clear that I have a manorial title in Hertfordshire, perhaps it may be wise to change my name at each inn I frequent."

Chapter 88

"I do believe that was my wife's coach but I couldn't be sure in these icy conditions and heavy snow. There are so many coaches on the road today, I cannot distinguish one family crest from another. I shall stay at an inn where I am not known this time, although I shall ensure that it is frequented by the wealthy who will be knowledgeable about where Queen Mary and her court are residing now that they are coming South. In that way I shall know how I can become part of her household so that that will be another source of income.

Ah. This looks to be a fine inn that appreciates gentry. The Boar's Head. Yes, I'll give this the benefit of my custom."

***

"What a fine inn you have here. I only frequent the best of inns when I am in this part of England so I shall certainly take advantage of your splendid rooms again. Are you the Landlord? Good. I hear that Mary, Queen of Scots is travelling South. That is such a long and arduous journey for one so young. Have you heard tell of where she is now? Oh yes, I'm frequently here, in the North West as I'm going to be purchasing a substantial property in these parts. Of course, I have a manor house near London but, like many successful friends of Queen Elizabeth – oh yes, I go to court frequently – I wish to increase my number of properties. Only the other day, Bess – you know, Countess of Shrewsbury – invited me to Chatsworth. Sadly, I was unable to accept her kind hospitality as my manor house needed attention. This is such a beautiful part of the country that I am looking at several areas. Oh yes, of course, do serve this gentleman. May I buy a large glass of claret for you? You are most welcome. Do you play chess, Losing Loadum, One-and-Thirty or Picket? Yes, of course, let's play Hazard.

Chapter 89

Margory settled into the seat of the coach and closed her eyes. What a good friend Bess was proving to be, she thought. They had managed to have a short, quiet time together that morning when Bess had told her she would let her know if she heard any reports of either Arthur or Mary, Queen of Scots. She assumed Arthur was, once more, buying a property in the North West and would put his latest female friend in charge of it. Perhaps he may even have more children by this person. Margory neither knew nor cared now. What a pity he didn't appear to be living in Lancashire permanently. But how could he? He spent so much money that he needed to return to The Manor in Greenwillows to replenish his life style. If only he would stay away. She couldn't bear the thought of his taking to her bed again. And, of course, he was spreading the word throughout Hertfordshire that she was losing her mind. Bess had been utterly shocked when Margory had told her that. She had also been very practical, as Bess always was. She had advised that, should Arthur speak of that again, Margory was to send a message to her and she would tell her private physician to examine Margory. He would then give an official report on her state of mind so that, should Arthur take her to some sort of mental institution, Margory could show the report to the person in charge. Dear Bess. How wise she was, and how helpful. Margory just hoped that she would not need to take advantage of this very kind offer. But Arthur would do what Arthur wanted to do and step on whomever he thought was in his way.

She must also decide her best course of action as far as dear Henry was concerned. When they had clung to each other at their departure from Chatsworth, it had torn her apart to see his little, sad face. Of course, she herself knew exactly why he couldn't return to The Manor. But Henry was only a child. All he could understand was that he was being separated from his own mother. Margory couldn't bear the thought of his not knowing why this was happening. She couldn't bear the thought of his assuming that it was because his own mother didn't love him, however strongly Marion assured him to the contrary. The fact was, he was living in one house while his mother lived in another and they rarely saw each other. How could he possibly understand that his mother had his best interests at heart when allowing this separation? He couldn't. Margory could only pray that, one day, he would understand it was the depth of his mother's love that was keeping them apart. How difficult to understand that, when love usually glued people together. But not this time. Margory's infinite love for her son must ensure his safety. And that meant his living under the roof of another for the moment. Margory could think of no other time in her life when her resolve had been so tested as now. Not even when she was accused of witchcraft. A tear escaped from her still closed eyes, but there was no tiny, fat finger to trace its journey.

Chapter 90

"My name? Ah yes, Landlord, of course, you require it for payment of my room. It is Lord Green. I don't think it's necessary for you to know where I usually reside, is it? Here is payment for two nights spent with you. Oh, it's not that I have anything to hide, my good man, of course I haven't. Other than the fact that I wish to buy a substantial property in these parts and would like it to be a surprise for my good wife. So the less I say, the better, don't you think.

I would be grateful, too, if you would keep me abreast of where the Queen of Scots is residing as, between us, my wife is of the old faith as is Mary – and of course you know that. You will also realise why I wish my questions to remain between us. While Queen Elizabeth's Attorney General plays the Protestant part while at court, when he returns to his lands here, he returns to being a Papist. But of course, you know that, too. Oh, don't worry, provided you keep my own secrets, nothing will escape my lips about yours, my good man.

Now, I was about to begin a card game of All Fours with my companion here. Oh, you're not familiar with it. Why don't we play dice, then? It is such a special game and I'm sure, like me, you enjoy it. Are you staying at this fine inn tonight? Oh, you're not. Well, that's a shame as I was looking forward to getting to know you a little better. You're part of Judge Gerard's household you say. I would like to get to know the judge while I'm here, so am hoping to be introduced to him some time. I am certainly very pleased to be making the acquaintance of people who are at the same level of society as I. I find it makes things so much easier, doesn't it. Allow me to buy you a drink. Landlord, another glass of whatever my estimable companion is drinking. What was your name again? Ah yes, I'm Lord Green from Hertfordshire.

Oh, you've heard that someone from Hertfordshire is frequenting these inns and cheating. How abominable! You just can't trust anyone these days, can you. Hertfordshire, of course, is a very large county. Now let us begin. Do you play chess, too?

Chapter 91

"Goodwife Sykes! How good it is to see you again. Is my husband at home? No? Well, I can't say that I'm disappointed about that as I have a great deal to do, having been away for some time. Let us retire to the hall where you can tell me everything that has happened since my departure for Chatsworth. First, are you well? Good.

"Oh, my husband put Lucy in charge of the household, did he and Thomas in charge of the estate. I see. Well, as my husband comes and goes without letting me know, that may be a good thing, as I won't need to trouble Master Hugh in future. I shall speak to Lucy when I have prayed and rested."

"Mistress Margory. I wasn't sure whether to tell you this, but as it was so very upsetting, I shall, knowing that you won't tell Master Arthur."

"What is it, Goodwife Sykes? Are you ill? Something of great concern to you – as I can see this is – is also a worry to me."

"In your absence, Mistress, when Master Arthur returned to find Master Hugh in charge of the estate, he was very angry indeed. Pardon me for saying this, Mistress, but your servants and I do know a little of your situation and, given that knowledge, I doubt that it was jealousy of Master Hugh that drove Master Arthur to say what he did and…"

"Yes, yes, Goodwife Sykes. Do get on. What is it? What happened while I was away?"

"Master Arthur was so incensed that he threatened to throw Lucy and Master Hugh in the cellar and lock them there, with the rats. I only mention this, Mistress, because I think, should Master Arthur carry out his threat, Lucy would either go mad or die of terror. You may know that she is afraid of the dark and, as for the rats…"

At that, Margory moved to sit beside Goodwife Sykes and, putting her arm around the elderly woman's shoulders, said,

"You have done exactly the right thing in telling me this, my dear and faithful servant. I shall think on't so that such a thing will not happen again. Oh, I'm not concerned for the safety of Master Hugh. Although he isn't as tall or broad as my husband, I am absolutely sure that he could take care of himself, whatever the situation. What concerns me, though, is that, as he would want to protect Lucy, he may, himself, because of that, have found himself in the cellar. That sort of behaviour will not happen again, I assure you. I shall take steps to make sure of that. However, I shall not tell you what I intend to do, as it will be better that you don't know. Now, I can see how very upset you have been and are about this, so you must go to your bed chamber. I shall tell Lucy to bring you refreshment and you must rest. I am so sorry that you have had to experience something so dreadful in my absence. Now go, and I shall not expect to see you again until the morning."

"Thank you, Mistress. I do, indeed, feel very tired."

Margory bit her lip to stop the tears as she watched her elderly servant drag her feet out of the library door. How could someone be so cruel as to threaten such a person. She needed to give this some thought but, in the meantime, she would ask for the Lord's guidance.

Chapter 92

"Lord Green, you say. And where, may I ask is your manor, sir?"

"It's a very fine manor in Hertfordshire and I intend to buy a similar estate in these parts, just as Sir Gilbert Gerard has done. Indeed, I'm looking forward to meeting him at one of the best inns some time."

"Are you indeed. Well, Sir Gilbert spends a great deal of time at court, of course. That is a grand ambition of yours and I wish you well with it. A warning, though, Lord Green. There are rumours of a vagabond who carries his own loaded dice and moves from one inn to another. He's said to be amassing a small fortune at the expense of other, reputable men, so I'd be careful if I were you."

"That's disgraceful. Thank you for telling me. I shall keep a watch out for such a person. Gentlemen such as you and I are unused to that sort of behaviour, of course, so let us continue with our game."

Putting his hand in his pocket, Arthur brought out unloaded dice and heaved a sigh of relief. What luck that this man had mentioned the way he usually played. It appeared that word was spreading about his activities. Perhaps he would need to visit taverns in addition to inns for a while. Shame, as the people who frequented taverns were not so high born and had less money to spend on gambling. However, if his means of getting rich was becoming known, he would need to be more careful. Yes, this had been a very helpful conversation with the gentleman. He would lie low for a while and consider his next step. Perhaps this would be a good time to approach Sir Francis Knollys. He had also heard that Sir Francis was to be in charge of the Scottish queen in the near future. Yes, this was perhaps the time to consider a different route to riches.

"That was a very enjoyable game, sir. One of the best I have had for some time. However, I am rather weary, having travelled from Hertfordshire in poor weather, so I shall retire to my bed. I am pleased to have made your acquaintance and shall look forward to another game soon."

"Indeed. And don't forget to be on the lookout for this cheat."

"I certainly shall not, and thank you for the warning."

Again, heaving a sigh of relief, Arthur thought how fortuitous that he should have received this warning, at this time. Yes, he must put away his special dice for the moment and pursue another path. Perhaps now would be an advantageous time to call upon the Countess at Chatsworth. So what if she was a friend of his wife's. Hadn't he received an invitation to join the Chatsworth Christmas festivities? That hadn't suited him, of course. He would buy another horse and fit himself out for such a visit. This Bess of Hardwick was known to have gained accountancy and management knowledge from her second husband which had resulted in her soaring wealth. Yes, he would prepare himself for such a visit.

"Landlord, my good man. I wish to send a message to the Countess of Shrewsbury, also known as Bess of Hardwick."

If the landlord appeared rather surprised, Arthur ignored it.

"Is the lady concerned a friend, sir?"

"Oh yes. I was unable to take up her kind offer of spending Christmas at Chatsworth, so shall make amends by calling on her in the next few days."

"I shall send my head stable hand with the message. He is very reliable and will respond well to your generosity, I know, sir."

The exchange of money sealed the arrangement.

Chapter 93

"Mistress Margory, a message has arrived from Chatsworth and the rider wishes to know if there is a reply."

"From Chatsworth? Oh, I wasn't expecting to hear from my friend, Bess, about Mary's travels South yet." Then, opening the message,

"Well, that is a surprise. My husband has contacted Bess to say that he would like to call upon her. What, I wonder, does he wish to speak to her about? I am certainly pleased that I was able to let the Countess know at Christmas what he is doing now. She wonders whether I know why he wishes to call – but I don't. I have absolutely no idea. But it will certainly be to further his own interests in some way. That is puzzling. She invites me to join them but, unfortunately, I shall have to decline as my management of this household has been delayed by my spending longer at Chatsworth at Christmas-time than I had intended, delightful as it was. No, I shall reply by asking her to let me know what, in fact, he wished to speak to her about. How very odd. I understood that he was spending time in the North West of the country where he was hoping to buy another manor, as he did several years ago. I do hope that he doesn't intend to ask my friend, Bess, for money. But no, if he does – which I think is unlikely – she is far too sensible to accede to such a request. So why is he visiting Chatsworth, and without me, his wife, when he knows very well that Bess and I are good friends. Ah yes, perhaps that is why. He is leaning on her friendship with me in order to make some sort of request. Because a request must certainly be the reason for his visit. How extraordinary!

Chapter 94

"How very kind of you to agree to see me, Countess. I know how fond of you my dear wife is. Also, I was very disappointed that I could not avail myself of your invitation to spend Christmas with you and your family. Had I been able to do that, I should certainly have done so. Will it be possible for me to also speak to your good husband, the Earl?"

The Countess's eyes widened.

"No, certainly not. The Earl is spending time at several of our estates, ensuring that Queen Mary will be comfortable wherever she is. Since travelling South, she has been under the guardianship of Sir Francis Knollys, both at Carlisle Castle and, now, at Bolton Castle. However, as Sir Francis is Treasurer of the Chamber, he cannot be expected to remain at those castles indefinitely. Consequently, my friend, Queen Elizabeth, has turned to my husband with the expectation that he will accommodate the queen at the most suitable of our estates."

"Oh, and where will the queen be residing, then?"

"Queen Elizabeth has not given her permission for us to divulge that information, certainly until plans are a little more firm. Do you have a particular reason for wanting to know, Master Arthur?"

"Oh no, no, but I think that my dear wife will be interested, of course, as she and Queen Mary are of the same faith."

"Indeed. And when Margory stayed with us at Christmas, we spoke of exactly that subject. When the time is appropriate, I hope that Margory will be able, once more, to come to Chatsworth so that we can arrange a suitable meeting. I, myself, expect to spend a little time with Queen Mary enjoying our needlework, so I am hoping that Margory and I can make that journey together. That is, of course, when it suits you and your household."

"I'm pleased that you keep that in mind, Countess, as my wife's management of the manor has not always been…"

"I'm sure Margory does what she can, when she can, particularly as The Manor has been in her family for several generations. I know that she is very fond of the estate and misses her parents greatly. But we shall not speak about that, as I understand you were not in Hertfordshire when they met their demise."

"Er no, I had bought another estate in the North West of the country at the time. As you say, it is better that we don't speak of that now as it was an extremely unhappy time for my dear wife."

Bess listened carefully to Arthur's description of the events and found it interesting to hear his own version of what had happened. He clearly did not think that Margory would have told her what, in fact, had happened at the time when she had needed her husband's support more than ever. How little he seemed to realise that good female friends opened their hearts to each other.

"Be that as it may," Bess continued, "you didn't give me the reason for this visit, Master Arthur."

"Ah no, and I thank you for seeing me without that knowledge. But I do think it would be more appropriate for me to have an audience with your husband, the Earl."

Bess patted her dress, irritated at this man's poor manners.

"I can assure you that, whatever the reason for your visit, I am perfectly capable of…Also, I am particularly busy at the moment."

"Of course, of course, how foolish of me. I am, once again, hoping to buy an estate in the North West and am accumulating the means by which I can do that."

At that, Bess turned to face him fully. Surely this man she had never met before was not about to ask for money?

Arthur flinched a little under the direct gaze of this wealthy, confident lady.

"I have heard that Queen Mary enjoys riding and I would be honoured to examine her stables so that I may see the best horses that can be bought. I, myself, have always enjoyed riding and horses. But, of course, I would need the introduction of an important person such as you or your husband, particularly as my own dear wife has not even yet made the acquaintance of Queen Mary. Do you think that would be possible?"

What an extraordinary person Margory's husband was, Bess thought. How had Margory ever found him to be attractive in any way at all?

Once again, Arthur shifted uneasily under the older woman's gaze. He wasn't used to being looked at in such a puzzled way. Perhaps it had not been a good idea, after all, to approach Margory's friend. How extraordinary, he thought, that such an obviously extremely wealthy woman, indeed, a woman who was known to be a friend of Queen Elizabeth, should conduct meetings such as this without the presence of her husband. How had she achieved her current status on her own, without her husband being in command of every move she made? He would need to watch Margory more carefully in case she began to adopt this same, confident, commanding demeanour when dealing with men. No, that wouldn't be right at all. And, of course, as the only child of the late Lord of the Manor, she had, previously, shown that tendency. Oh no, that would never do.

The Countess broke through his thoughts.

"When my husband returns, I shall speak to him about your request. However, he is an extremely busy man and, as I'm sure you realise, your request does not have the importance of many duties he is being called upon to carry out for Her Majesty, at the moment. I suggest that, when I have been able to speak to him, I send a message to Margory at The Manor in Hertfordshire. I cannot say, though, when that will be. I assume you are spending some time in Hertfordshire, are you?"

Again, Bess turned so that she was looking him fully in the face. She hoped he would realise that she did know a little about his conduct towards his wife. Although, of course, he would not know that she was aware of his despicable behaviour towards his child, too.

Putting on the smile that had been enjoyed by Margory all those years ago, Arthur said,

"Of course. I do thank you most sincerely, Countess, for seeing me. I shall await your message."

Chapter 95

Just a brief note to Margory would suffice.

"My dear friend. I thought it may be helpful for you to know that your husband has requested, what amounted to, an audience with the Scottish Queen. He said that he has an interest in horses and would like to see her stables. Quite frankly, Margory, I found his request to be odd and can only assume that he was not telling me everything he has in mind. I'm sure, too, that you will be amused to hear he was clearly of the impression that I should not be dealing with his request, and that it should be made directly to my husband, the Earl. I noted his surprise when I assured him that he could rely on his audience being with me. Suffice to say that I found it interesting to meet your husband!"

Chapter 96

1568

As Arthur took the carriage north once more, his thoughts returned to his meeting with the Countess of Shrewsbury. Who would have thought that a lowly woman would be allowed to conduct such a meeting with himself, a Lord of the Manor, about to become Lord of a second. As the Countess was a friend of his wife's, he would need to ensure that Margory did not begin to behave in the same way. Yes, the way he treated his wife would certainly have to continue, if not to increase in severity, although he could not punish her as much as he would like now that his son was no longer living at The Manor. It had always been such a pleasure to see the pain he inflicted on her increase when he turned to beating his son. He was his son, after all, and he would treat him exactly as he pleased. But where could Henry be? Obviously, his wife did not know. How stupid the woman was. How could anyone lose their own child? Particularly a child they loved dearly. He would give this more thought. First, he would force Margory to give him another child. Force would clearly be needed once again. Besides, he quite enjoyed the power of making her do something she didn't want to do. Once he had succeeded in doing that, he would, once more, look into putting her into an institution for the mentally deranged. In the meantime, he would continue to gain money from foolish people who failed to realise how easy it is to play games in a different way.

He didn't need the Countess of high-and-mighty Shrewsbury anyway. He would do as he had done so many years ago when commanded to enter The Manor by the back, servants' entrance. He would go to Bolton Castle where, not only did his talkative game players tell him the Scottish queen was residing but, if he was fortunate, he may well find Sir Francis Knollys at home, too. Oh yes, gone were the days of his being treated as a servant. He was so close now to buying a second manor house that he would watch out for a woman who would be its mistress. This time, he would be very careful to choose someone who would do his bidding when he snapped his fingers. One who wouldn't need to be forced into enjoying time in the bedchamber with him. Here he was in Bolton. Gentlemen in The Olde Man & Scythe could, he was sure, have their tongues loosened to divulge how he could gain access to Bolton Castle. Someone had told him it had a substantial maze so, if necessary, he would walk around that so that he could watch who came and went.

Chapter 97

The word was that Bolton had been given permission to hold a market hundreds of years ago. That would be an excellent place for me to buy provisions, at the same time asking where Bolton Castle is. Stall holders were bound to be impressed that I wished to speak to Sir Francis Knollys. They would have no idea that we had never met and that it was only because he is Treasurer of the Chamber that I wished to speak to him. At last, here is the Olde Man & Scythe.

"Take my carriage and horses. I shall be here for some time."

Then, striding into the inn.

"My good man, I hear that your cellars have the finest wine and ale. First, show me to your best rooms. As I intend to purchase a large estate in these parts, I wish to visit Sir Francis.

This statement was met by a puzzled frown.

"Why, Sir Francis Knollys, of course. Is there another such great Sir Francis in the area? No, I think not. Of course, we haven't yet met, but I intend to rectify that at the first opportunity. First, I would like to partake of a bottle of your best claret before dining. I have just arrived in Bolton, having had an audience at Chatsworth. Oh yes, I cannot always accept when invited so wanted to make amends. Of course, I was disappointed that the Earl had been called away by our good Queen Elizabeth to ensure that his many castles are ready to accommodate the Scottish queen, when needed. But no doubt our paths will cross when I return to my manor in Hertfordshire. Of course, in the Earl's absence, I enjoyed an audience with the Countess. But I shall not linger further on that, less important conversation, however impressive that lady is. Now, where is that claret?"

Chapter 98

"My good man. How far is Castle Bolton? Yes, I mean the castle, not the village, although that will do. Thank you. I shall stable my horses at the nearest inn and shall then message Sir Francis Knollys. What do you mean, he's having difficulty persuading the Scottish Queen to come south? Oh, I see, she thinks England means imprisonment. Well, from what I have seen of the portraits, she has the Scots red hair so I imagine she has a temper to go with that feature. Although my thoughts are to remain between us. I understand she enjoys riding, so I shall endeavour to look at her stables. I've heard tell that this Castle Bolton has very high walls so it certainly sounds like a prison. No, no, let us turn to the more pleasant topic of the games that I shall play here. I enjoy several and would appreciate your introducing me to one of your patrons who may be willing to teach me chess. All I know – and I deem this as strange – is that the Queen, originally a weak piece at the beginning of the 15th century, and quite rightly so, became dominant towards the end of that century. How could that be? I regard that as very strange. Where will the empowerment of women end?

Chapter 99

"My dear Goodwife Sykes, how are you today? I think I may go for a ride. It's such a beautiful day that I feel like riding with the wind in my hair. In my husband's absence, and with the help of yourself and the servants, I think the manor is well organised now. I have given you a daily timetable of when I may need your aid and when I would like you to rest. Please don't forget to rest, will you. Cook has a month's listing of the meals we shall be enjoying and, with your help, the other servants know what their duties are on a daily basis. I have also spoken to Lucy regarding her teaching her two children what they need to know. She will be doing that in the nursery and is delighted that I am showing an interest in children whom others, in the circumstances, may well have decided to ignore. Under her guidance, they are becoming charming children.

So, with all going well around me, I feel the need for fresh air and freedom and shall go where my horse takes me. As my husband's location is unknown and as I know not when he will return, I shall enjoy doing exactly as I please, when I please, at the moment. In the unlikely event that he returns when I am gone, please tell him that I am out riding, you know not where and shall be returning shortly. I am well aware, my dear woman, how very diplomatic you are, and for that I thank you. Now, please ask Thomas to bring my favourite horse, Facebelle, to the front of The Manor and I shall be gone. Take care of yourself in my absence, and, remember, do rest."

Diary entry: It has been quite some time since I rode with no destination in mind. However, a delightful thought popped into my mind. It was Christmas at Chatsworth when I last saw my dear son and great friend, Marion. Yes, that is where I shall go. Marion and I have such a good friendship that I know she will be perfectly happy for me to call on her, unannounced. Of course, I shall initially remain some distance from the cottage in case Henry and Jacob should be playing outside. I could not bear to hurt my darling child any more than he has been hurt already, particularly as he knows not why we must remain apart, for the moment. Yes, I shall leave now and take tea with my good friend. I find it very helpful to have this diary and am glad that no-one, not even Goodwife Sykes, knows of its existence, nor its hiding place. It is such a pleasure to be able to write down my own, personal thoughts, when I'm thinking them. But they are my thoughts and, under no circumstances do I wish them to be divulged. That makes them even more precious. Now I shall leave to visit my good friend.

Margory's diary entries were interrupted by knocking on the library door.

"What is it, Goodwife Sykes? Has my husband returned? Oh there's a message for him. Well, just leave it… It's not for him, but for me? Please ask the rider to wait in the event of the sender requiring a reply."

Chapter 100

Opening the message, Margory saw that it was from Bess, asking her to visit at a time that would be convenient for her. How fortuitous she thought, that the message should arrive just as she was about to visit Marion and see Henry. That would allow her to talk to her friend about her possible absence and where she was going. Yes, Margory felt very pleased about this coincidence and, writing a reply, asked Goodwife Sykes to invite the messenger in so that he could rest awhile and have a light meal, should he wish, before returning.

Margory then mounted her horse and left, her flying hair echoing her lightness of spirit at the thought of seeing her dearly beloved son as well as discussing with Marion what she and Abner had been doing. Having received Bess's message, she would also be able to tell Marion about her intended visit to Chatsworth in order to hear the latest news, not only of Bess, but Mary, Queen of Scots. How very exciting that would be, she thought. However, Margory realised that she needed to heed Bess's words regarding discretion in the exercise of her faith and discussion of it with Queen Mary. She regarded Bess to be such a good, wise friend, that she would be guided by her. But Margory knew, too, that she would welcome the opportunity of getting to know Queen Mary, even if only to discuss their faith. Margory's faith always had been, and would continue to be very important to her. At the same time, however, she needed to keep in mind her father's words. How she missed her father's wise counsel.

Chapter 101

"Yes, I realise that I have been given Baron Scrope's own apartments. However, only 30 of my men and six ladies-in-waiting can stay here at Bolton Castle. I know not where the rest are… Oh, they are in lodgings nearby. Well they're of no use to me there, are they. I need all my 51 knights, servants and ladies-in-waiting where I can tell them how they can help me, when. I have never, in my entire life, been served by so few cooks and grooms. Yes, I know I have my hairdresser on hand – how could I not. And yes, my apothecary, physician and surgeon are with me, too. It's just too annoying. This castle is entirely unsatisfactory for a person of my status. What do I mean? What do I mean? What about tapestries? What about rugs? And how can I live with so little furniture?"

Sir Francis Knollys waited patiently for this tirade to end.

"Your Majesty…"

"Oh, you do acknowledge, my status then. If so, why have I been moved to this dreary castle. As though Carlisle Castle wasn't bad enough, I'm now imprisoned here…"

"Not imprisoned, Your Majesty. These are fair lands about which you are allowed…

"Allowed! Well, I am very fortunate to be allowed, am I not."

"If you would let me finish, your Majesty. These are fair lands about which you are able to wander. There is also a fine park as well as a series of deer parks surrounded by high walls. So, rather than being imprisoned, Your Majesty, I know you will understand that your safety is our main concern. The castle also overlooks the Forest of Wensleydale which is well stocked with game. Not only that, but you may hunt when you wish."

At the sound of hunting, the Scottish queen's impatience abated somewhat.

"Also, Queen Elizabeth has, herself, loaned some pewter vessels as well as a copper kettle, as she does wish your stay here to be as comfortable as possible."

"Well, you can tell Her Majesty that, as we're fairly closely related, pewter vessels and a copper kettle are the least I expect. Thank the Lord my friend, Mary Seton, still remains to take care of my hair."

"Not only that, your Majesty, you will be taught English so that your language expertise is broadened from its current French, Latin and Scots."

"Well, I suppose that may be of help to me, now that I'm in England. And what about my faith? The true faith. How am I to worship the Lord in the way I must? Answer that, then, if you can. How long must I stay here?"

"I know not, at the moment, Your Majesty, but, perhaps about six months. And I'm very sorry but the less we say about your faith, the better, too."

"Six months! Without all my knights, servants and ladies-in-waiting! I really do protest. Please tell your Queen Elizabeth that I am very unhappy. Where does she intend to have me sent next?"

"There's talk of Tutbury, but the decision isn't final yet. I suggest you inspect your stables as you may wish to offer employment to more stable hands. That would make your presence here more pleasing to the villagers of Castle Bolton who are already watching to see what Your Majesty intends to do."

"Well. In that case, I shall take on more stable hands. I have no wish to displease the villagers. My imprisonment is not due to them, after all."

With a sigh, Sir Francis turned, leaving the lady with her remonstrances.

Chapter 102

"My dear Margory, how wonderful to see you! An unexpected surprise. Henry and Jacob are playing around the other side of the cottage at the moment, Henry is very well and is beginning to mention you a little less now. I don't want that to disturb you, my dear. He's far from forgetting you but I thought it would be unwise to mention you on his birthday in June, for example. He's only three, of course, and, while he won't forget you entirely, as he isn't seeing you regularly, his memory will fade. But only a little, my dear."

Margory brushed away a tear. How could she bear it if Henry were to forget her entirely? She couldn't. But she must always, always think about what would be best for him, not herself. Here, with Marion keeping him safe and with Jacob fast becoming his good friend, he was in excellent hands. His safety was her paramount concern and always would be. She simply would not risk his being subjected to Arthur's cruelty any further. Just the thought of it made Margory straighten her shoulders. Now that she was seeing Arthur less, it would be fairly easy to forget the dreadful way he had treated his son. How could a father behave in that way? Well, she knew the answer to that, of course. He did it to display his power. He also did it to hurt her in a way he knew was the greatest punishment she could endure. When Arthur returned, she would do her best to follow his wishes. That wouldn't be easy. In fact, she would find it extremely difficult. However, she would try very hard to ask cook to prepare his favourite food, she would try to engage him in the sort of conversation he would enjoy and she would show an interest in what he was doing in North West England. Yes, that's what she would do. The one thing she could not, absolutely could not do, though, was to succumb to him in bed. That would just be a step too far. In fact, many steps too far. He had hurt her so very much in the past when, not only had he been disloyal to her late parents – and that was in spite of her father's having treated him very well - but had shown no concern about her safety at all in leaving her for so long. Four years he had stayed away, only to return when he was impecunious. And then there was his infidelity with Lucy. Also, of course, at the back of her mind – and Margory tried very hard to keep the thoughts in that place – there was her fondness for Hugh. It mattered not that she could not indulge those emotions. But exist they did. Thank goodness she had been strong enough to not take things further. No, her faith told her that would be wrong. And it was. Margory bit her lip so hard she tasted blood.

"My dear, you looked far away. What is on your mind? I shall ask Abner to bring the boys to the front of the cottage so that you can see them easily, but they won't see us. In particular, as Henry wasn't expecting to see you, he will be enjoying playing with Jacob."

It was then that Margory decided she wouldn't let Henry know that she was here. Their parting would be too upsetting. Yes, she would stay out of sight while watching her dearly beloved son enjoying himself. Excusing herself, Margory put her face in her hands and wept while Marion put her arm around her friend's shoulder, knowing she could do no more about this very sad situation.

Chapter 103

"What a bright, sunny day it is, my good man, and still quite hot. Rather than take my coach, I shall ride to Bolton Castle. I so rarely have time to enjoy our fair countryside that, yes, that's what I shall do. I know not when I shall return, but I expect it will be some time next week. Please leave my belongings in my room – which I shall, of course, pay for, albeit in my absence – and keep it locked at all times."

"Of course. I'm sure I don't need to tell you, your Lordship, but, as you are so well dressed and intend to ride, I would suggest that you do not carry anything of worth lest you meet those who would wish you ill."

"Yes, I agree. Thank you. I am so used to dressing in this way, naturally, and usually take a coach, perhaps, in fact, I should change into the clothes I wear when walking my land in Hertfordshire. Yes, that is what I shall do."

What Arthur did not mention was that he would, as always, carry his wheel lock pistol. Very few were familiar with a gun that could be loaded and locked to use when needed. He recalled how very useful it had been in seeing off thieves before he and Margory were married. How impressed the Lady of the Manor had been! That had certainly served to endear him somewhat to Margory's mother who, until that time, had been very condescending towards him.

Suddenly, Arthur realised that, in fact, the suggestion of less smart clothing would serve more than one purpose. He would leave his horse a little way off, then enter the maze at Bolton Castle and watch who came and went. He would also try to find the stables so that he could then speak to the head groom at the castle about becoming a stable hand.

Just then, his thoughts returned to The Manor in Hertfordshire, all those years ago, recalling how boldly he had knocked on its front door and been told he should go to the rear entrance as he was a mere servant. That is exactly what he would do now so that he could find out what was happening inside the castle with its very high walls. It was always the servants who knew what was going on. It was always the servants who gossiped – well, usually. For now, he would find the castle, walk through the maze and look for the stables. In that way, he could plan what he would do the following day. While he was dressed in informal clothes, he could get inside the castle, talk to the other servants and see if stable hands were needed. After all, he had discovered that people were very superficial. If you were wearing servants' clothes, you were treated like a servant; when you wore clothes that were fitting to the Lord of the Manor, you were treated accordingly.

At that moment, Arthur had an idea. In this part of England, away from his manorial duties, he could play the part of two people, purely by dressing differently. He also knew how to speak differently, of course, thanks to his high-born lady wife. When she had started his lessons, he had spoken like a servant, with the vocabulary of a servant. But once he had risen through the ranks at The Manor, he had begun to speak differently and dress differently as well as learning the manners of the high-born. The fact that he still preferred the company of other, more lowly born, was irrelevant. The fact was, he had the ability to move between the two levels of society. And that is what he would do now. He'd nearly forgotten that. What a long time ago it was. Of course, he would have to be careful. Once more, he was accumulating money by playing certain games in a certain way. A way that may be discovered, if he wasn't careful. He was doing that as a Lord of the Manor whereas his entry to Bolton Castle would be as a servant. However, he intended to get to know as many people who lived there as possible.

He'd heard that Queen Mary may not be staying there very long. That would make it easier for him to change from servant to potential Lord of the Manor, somewhere in these parts. Although, if the Scottish queen were to move on, he would make sure he learned her new destination. Who knew? He might even meet her. Hadn't his looks and smile attracted Margory all those years ago? And how much more sophistication did he have at his disposal now, should he decide to use it. Although he would need to be careful, he would change from servant to Lord of the Manor whenever it suited the occasion. Arthur grinned. How clever he was to be able to change from one character to another.

Chapter 104

"Goodwife Sykes. I'm going to accept the Countess's invitation and shall take our coach to Chatsworth tomorrow while the weather remains warm. I have noticed, though, as we progress through the Autumn months, that the evenings are becoming colder. As you know, The Manor is in good order and you and I have spent time with Cook arranging meals for the next month. I shall speak to Lucy about making sure everything runs well in my absence and that of my husband because, once again, I know not where he is nor when he will return. Should he come back while I'm away, would you let him know that I shall be gone for about two weeks so shall expect to return some time in November, provided that is convenient to the Countess. I shall tell Lucy all that you and I have arranged at The Manor and that I would like her to work with you in ensuring that everything runs smoothly. After all, while she and my husband lived in the North West of England, she ran what I understand was a sizeable manor house there, so she has some experience. However, I know, too, that she will welcome your advice and help. What I do insist upon, too, my dear friend, is that you take time to rest, each and every day. Even if only for an hour. You will do that, won't you? I shall also tell Thomas of my absence and that he will be in charge of the estate, as before, when my husband commanded."

"Your ladyship is too kind. Yes, I shall rest when I can, in your absence."

"No, Goodwife Sykes. You will definitely rest every day in my absence. Is that clear? Not only when you can."

Chapter 105

"My dear Margory, how glad I am that you could visit. Catherine will take you to your bedchamber and will stay with you to unpack your cases. Do rest a while and join me later this afternoon."

"How are you, Bess? I do thank you for sending the message regarding my husband's visit, about which I knew nothing until I heard from you. As I rarely see him, I have no idea what he had in mind when visiting you. And as for requesting an audience with the Earl, having given no notification of the reason for his visit, I am lost for words. However, I do know my husband very well. I am sorry to say that he respects nothing and no-one, particularly ladies. Were it not for the fact that my parents ensured that I was educated well and gained in confidence under their care, Arthur's treatment of me, and, of course, of our son, would, I think drive me to madness. Indeed, when I do see him, he implies that he will arrange for me to be institutionalised."

"As I said previously, my dear, we'll see about that! In a way I am not surprised as, when he visited Chatsworth, he made it very clear that he was only interested in an audience with the Earl. So I needed to inform him that that is not the way this household is run. I didn't add that, for a man such as he, irrespective, my dear, of the fact that he is your husband, he would need to accept an audience with me. While I know you fairly well, I don't know him at all. Anyway, I enjoy your company too much, Margory, to allow the behaviour of your husband to spoil your visit. Knowing you and your family as I do, and now that I know your husband a little, it does surprise me that you married him in the first place, although he is a good looking man. But that was some time ago and cannot be changed. Now, let me tell you why I invited you to Chatsworth."

Listening to what her friend had to say, Margory totally understood why Bess saw no good in Arthur. Indeed, as time went on, she, who had always been able to find a small part of her heart still warmed to Arthur, could understand that. However, that place in her heart had closed totally when Arthur had beaten his baby. That, she could not and would not tolerate, even to the point of not seeing her dear child herself. Henry's safety was all that mattered. Also, while Margory could understand her friend's lack of understanding of why she had married Arthur, Bess, of course, was unaware of what it had been like to be the plain daughter of a Lord of the Manor. She was unaware of how it felt to have her gentlemen peers greet her then turn away for conversation with more attractive young ladies. But that was a long time ago. She would not allow those thoughts to mar her visit to her friend.

"Margory. Have you heard a word I've said?"

"I'm so sorry, Bess. Any mention of my husband takes me back to when we first met, when all I saw was a handsome young man."

"Yes, I agree. He is good looking, but, internally, he appears to be one of the most unattractive people I have ever met. As such, he doesn't deserve our devoting any more time to speaking about him."

"So, let us turn to the reason why I am very glad that you could visit at this time. It is connected to the Scottish queen's presence in England. Oh, I can see our discussion about Queen Mary is to be further delayed. Here are two of my dear daughters whom you met during your visit at Christmas. Elizabeth, Mary: I know you will remember my friend, Mistress Margory, who stayed with us at Christmas. Yes, that's right, she was here with her friends and adorable, little son, Henry. Are you going to join us for tea? Good. I can see, Margory, that we shall need to wait until the new day dawns to have our conversation. Probably just as well as you will be more rested tomorrow. Now girls, tell Mistress Margory and me how you have spent your day."

Margory, in fact, was quite relieved to have had the subject of Arthur interrupted as it continued to pain her. Bess was right, really. How could she have entered marriage vows with one so totally ambitious that he cared not who he hurt when climbing the social ladder. How could she have played the very large part she had in that climb? But wisdom in hindsight was so very easy. After all, she, herself, had mainly harboured selfish thoughts. She had intended to make Arthur hers and had ensured that nothing and nobody got in her way. Really, it was only at the birth of Henry that she had begun to be totally devoted to someone else although, of course, part of her heart lay elsewhere. Now, of course, the past had caught up with her in the shape of what had previously been a very self-centred husband who was now utterly cruel. That step seemed to be a very small one. His one redeeming feature was that he had, in fact, loved another. How could she have been so blind as not to have seen what was happening right before her eyes? No, Arthur was not all bad, just as she, herself, was not all good. Perhaps the Lord had introduced her to Hugh in order to test just how good or bad she really was – "Lead me not into temptation." So far, she was succeeding in not breaking her marriage vows. But that was very difficult, in spite of the fact that she rarely saw him. But she did not wish to see him more often, in fact, as she could not bear to witness the dreadful way in which Arthur treated him. His insinuations were so very insulting to a man of Hugh's high character. She still could not believe that her feelings were reciprocated. But that appeared to be the case. And how wonderfully warm that made her feel.

Chapter 106

Arthur stopped in his tracks. Although he was still some way off from the Bolton castle's vast acres, his admiration was tinged with envy. He knew a little about the history of the castle, but arithmetic and finances were his main interest in life, not history. He knew the high-walled building before him – although quite some distance away and surrounded by parks and gardens – was about 200 years old. He also knew – from his dice fellow players – that there was a series of deer parks and that was a sure sign of high society. Although Arthur was very ambitious, he knew that these walls and these owners were too high for him to even consider joining their ranks. No, he was already Lord of one manor and a second would suffice, in this part of the country.

As he began to walk towards the walls, and although not interested in plants, flowers or vegetables, even his nostrils could not ignore the delightful smells of an array of flowers, the like of which he had never encountered before. How very pretty it all was, as well as being extremely grand. At the Hertfordshire manor, he left the organisation of the gardens to his wife. However, from the little he did know, these were globe flowers of many colours, poppies, clove pinks and periwinkle. And how wonderful was the perfume of the roses. Arthur was impressed. He would speak to his wife to ensure that the manor's gardens carried these blooms, too. After all, he may have to sell the Hertfordshire manor house if, one day, he found himself even more penurious than he was now. Yes, Arthur was dazzled and couldn't wait to explore the forests and deer parks further. Suddenly, he stopped and looked again at what he knew to be the crenels of the castle. Wasn't that an archer he had seen? He must take care. After all, from what he had been told, both by the Countess of Shrewsbury and in Castle Bolton, the Scottish queen was virtually a prisoner in England. Although he cared not what her status might be, he needed to keep in mind that, while this castle was very beautiful, it was also a fortress and, at the moment, it was holding a Queen within its walls. What if he should meet her? He would smile his enigmatic smile. That always worked for women. But no. He needed to be sensible – never his strong point – and realise that she would be accompanied by many servants wherever she went. While he would walk with confidence around these grounds, he would also need to keep in mind that Mary was a Queen. Yes, he needed to remember his main mission here. He was dressed like a servant and his presence was due to the fact that he loved horses and would like to serve in Her Majesty's stables. Or perhaps they were referred to as the stables of Sir Richard Scrope. Whatever, he would be looking into increasing his wealth by becoming a stable hand. And, if he could gain an audience with Sir Francis Knollys, perhaps he could secure a loan, too. The sooner he found the servants' entrance, the better, as he felt quite vulnerable in this unknown part of the world, faced by this magnificent castle.

Perfect. There was a gardener. "Hello, my man. How clever you are to know so much about these many varieties of flowers, herbs and vegetables."

"I know nowt about vegetables and 'erbs. I'm one of t'undreds of gardeners 'ere who taks care of some of't flowers. And 'oo are you, may I ask? Never seen you around 'ere before. Does tha know we've got a queen staying 'ere. I wouldn'a want to be you if any of them archers see you wanderin' around."

Arthur shuffled. Exactly what he had been thinking. This man did speak in a strange way. Must be something to do with this being the North of England.

"No. I came to the village asking for work. I've been working as a stable hand as, just as you like your plants, I love horses. Have you heard tell that stable hands might be needed here?"

"Tha doesna talk like us do around 'ere either. Where is thee from, then?"

"Oh, you could say that I'm from a few places, really. 'ertfordshire (Arthur tried to copy the man's way of talking in the hope that he would open up a little) and over Lancashire way. I like to travel around a bit tha knows."

"Ay well, we're not much for foreigners in these parts. But you sound as though you may be all reet."

"Thank you. Would tha mind showin' me the servants' entrance and I'll leave you to get on with your fine work."

"Follow me."

And that is exactly what Arthur did, without even a smile having to crack his lips. In fact, he had the feeling that this man who spoke oddly wouldn't be taken in by a smile. This may be a bit more of a challenge than he had realised.

Chapter 107

"Well, Margory, alone at last. Although I love my large family dearly, it is sometimes very pleasant to converse with another adult friend, such as yourself. Now, the reason I invited you was to let you know what is happening to the Scottish Queen. She is currently – er – being taken care of, shall we say, at Bolton Castle and it's thought that she will remain there for about six months. My husband, the Earl, has been given the honour by Her Majesty, Queen Elizabeth, of making ready another of our castles, for Queen Mary's on-going stay in England. That may be Tutbury. I think it will be much more to Queen Mary's liking as it is larger, so will hold her whole court which Bolton Castle cannot. It will also be much more convenient for my husband, the Earl, as it is only about half the distance from Chatsworth that Bolton Castle is. I expect to be joining her in a few days to do some embroidery and would like you to come with me. Would you like that?"

"That would, indeed, be an honour, Bess, but my embroidery skills are not as good as yours. What did you have in mind?"

"Well, I alluded to this during your last visit, Margory. Queen Mary and yourself are of the same faith and I think it would be pleasurable for Her Majesty to speak to you. She hasn't, after all, been in this country very long and, I'm sure, will be feeling rather lonely, in spite of being surrounded by some of her court. Although she speaks several languages, she is being taught English and that will make her feel more relaxed, I hope. Also, her faith, I know, is very important to her, and you share that with her. You will, however, recall my saying that Queen Elizabeth feels very strongly that the Scottish Queen should not be allowed to spread her faith in England. That means it is absolutely essential that any conversation you have with her must be carried out in private, with no-one else there at all. That may not be easy – indeed, it may not be possible - as, of course, she always has a number of ladies-in-waiting attending her. After I have introduced you to Her Majesty, I shall tell her that you and she have something in common which is important to both of you. However, as she is now residing in this country as a guest of Queen Elizabeth, any conversation that you and she have on the subject must remain totally confidential, between the two of you. If she is unwilling to allow this, then such a conversation must not take place. As it is, I shall not be telling my husband, the Earl, about it. He is trying very hard to carry out Queen Elizabeth's wishes in arranging one of our castles so that Queen Mary will be as comfortable as possible in this country. And that isn't easy. She is, after all, a member of the royal family who is used to being surrounded by luxury and many servants. It is only because this is not proving to be very easy for the Earl to arrange that I think a private conversation with you about a subject that is dear to both your hearts may be welcomed, not only by Queen Mary, but also you, yourself, my dear."

Margory listened intently to what Bess was saying and knew exactly what she meant. It took her back to that extremely sad evening when she had been invited to join her parents for supper. At the time, she had, of course, been experiencing difficulties with Arthur, in their early days of marriage, and had not given a thought to the fact that her parents were regarded as recusants which would not be tolerated. She recalled the dreadful shock of what her father was telling her. She remembered, too, that her first reaction and instinct had been to tell her parents that she could not live without them and that she would join them in death. How selfish a thought that had been. Of course, her father – wise to the end – had told her that he and her mother could not go to the stake – a means of execution requested by her father so that they would leave this earth together - knowing that their only child would also be executed. He had gone on to tell her, firmly but gently, that she must promise to worship in private, without telling anyone else – not one single person – how she would worship and where. That evening, that last supper with her parents, had left her grief-stricken. And, of course, at the time, she had no knowledge of her husband's activities which had rendered her without his support. Yes, she knew exactly what Bess meant in saying that no-one else must know. She trusted Bess implicitly and knew that she had both her and Queen Mary's best interests at heart when telling her that this subject and any conversation surrounding it must remain between the two of them. This was one exception Margory knew her father would understand. How very sorry she was that faith should produce such problems. Why couldn't everyone accept each other's way of worship and, who knows, even join together from time to time in praising God. But no, now she was going too far. What a foolish thought.

"Yes, Bess. I totally agree that any conversations that Queen Mary and I may have must remain between the two of us. I understand the importance of that secrecy, but I do wonder whether the Scottish Queen will accept and adhere to it."

"Margory. As I said, before you and she meet in private, I shall absolutely ensure that Queen Mary understands that such a conversation will not be allowed unless it is held in private. She may decline, of course, as, at no time is she ever alone. Now let us think about when we shall go to Bolton Castle and what we shall wear. I shall also take some gifts which will be from both of us. Additionally, I think it would be wise to make this journey when my husband is at Tutbury – if you see what I mean. He is shouldering the responsibilities that Queen Elizabeth has asked of him, but it isn't easy and I do not intend to burden him further."

There had, in the past, been times when Margory was particularly impressed by the Countess's kindness and wisdom. This was yet another such occasion. She felt very fortunate to have her as a friend.

Chapter 108

"Thank you very much for your help, my man. What is your name, by the way? And who is this fine lady?"

"I'm John Thomas and this is our very good cook, Agnes."

"Who is this, then, and what're you doin' 'ere?" Once again, Arthur's presence was questioned and he realised he had to be very careful in his explanations.

"My name is Arthur, I'm a groom and I'm wondering whether more stable 'ands are being taken on, 'ere. What a delicious smell. I bet you're a very good cook and…"

"You're not going to wriggle your way into tastin' my bakin'. Not yet anyway. I'll see if the 'ousekeeper is anywhere to be seen. 'Er name's Mrs Belton. Does she know you're comin'? No, well, you'd best take a seat out in't 'allway until we know whether she or anyone else can see you. What did you say your name is?"

"Arthur Wright. Thank you."

As the cook waddled away, Arthur realised that being included in any gossip among the servants here may not be as easy as he had originally thought. They seemed more reserved than he was used to in Hertfordshire – friendly enough, but reserved. But then, he and his parents had always been known at The Manor in Hertfordshire, so that situation was entirely different. Ah, here came quite an imperious looking woman. Must be the main housekeeper here. He'd see whether his smile broke any ice with her.

"You're Master Wright, I'm told. Did anyone know you were coming? Well, you were taking quite a foolish chance as we have a special guest who is being guarded day and night. Our Head Butler, George, can't see anybody at the moment. Why have you come here, unannounced, did they say?"

"I do apologise for inconveniencing you and the household, Mrs Belton, but I've been travelling around this part of the country for some time in the hope of finding work, and heard tell that Bolton Castle may be hiring stable hands. Is that right?"

"The person you should speak to is the man in charge of the stables."

Calling to a servant girl who happened to be passing, the housekeeper said, "Anne. Take this man out to the stables. He wants a job there. Yes, stop what you're doin' for the moment. As you can see, Master Wright, turnin' up without an appointment was most unwise of you."

Not to be deterred, Arthur smiled brilliantly at the pretty young servant girl who suddenly appeared rather flustered. This was more like it, he thought. This good looking young thing was going to be the start of his finding out what this household was like and even whether the Scottish Queen went out hunting. If she did, that would mean the horses would be very fine. Everything in good time.

"Come with me," she said softly, and blushing, Arthur noticed.

Nodding to both the cook and housekeeper who were already returning to their duties, Arthur looked at the servant.

"And what did they say your name is, you lovely girl? Was it Anne? Pretty name for a pretty young thing."

"Oh sir. You do talk nice. You're not from around 'ere, are you?"

Just for a moment, Arthur had forgotten that all these servants spoke differently, in a way he hadn't heard before. He would need to speak as they did sometimes so that they felt comfortable when confiding in him.

"I'm from everywhere, really. Tell me about yourself. 'Ow long 'ave you been workin' 'ere? Is it a nice place to work? What are the other servants like?"

"This is the first time I've worked in such a grand place as this. Don't you think it's lovely? So big, I've lost count of 'ow many bedchambers there are. Everybody seems really friendly and nice."

"And do you 'ave a bedchamber 'ere, in the castle, or do you go back to your mother and father at the end of a day?"

"My dad ran off a year ago and my mam died. So I've got nobody. But I'm makin' some friends 'ere."

Thinking this all sounded rather familiar, Arthur began to relax. Putting an arm around the girl's shoulders, he said,

"I'm very sorry to 'ear that."

Again, the girl blushed, but didn't withdraw, Arthur noticed. This girl would certainly be where he would start in getting to know what happened in a huge castle such as this when a member of the royal family was in residence. He would perhaps need to take things a little more slowly than usually, though.

"'Ere's our man in charge of 't stables. Thomas. This gentleman – er – man wants to speak to you about bein' a stable 'and. I've got to get back now. Then, glancing down shyly, "P'raps see you again."

Using that ever-helpful smile, Arthur looked at her, "I certainly 'ope so. Thanks for your 'elp."

Arthur turned back to the man called Thomas.

"I've 'eard tell that stable 'ands are wanted 'ere. Is that right?"

"How much work 'ave you done with 'orses before, what kind of 'orses and where?"

Arthur relaxed. This was familiar ground. He had always loved horses and been able to manipulate the ladies. It was all going very well now. Suddenly, his attention was drawn to a magnificent coach arriving – at the main entrance, of course. Arthur wondered who it was. Perhaps he could get closer to take a look at the coat of arms. Turning to the Head Groom, Arthur asked,

"A very fine coach." Then, in order not to sound inappropriately curious, he turned to him and said,

"Who is it, I wonder? I s'pose you're used to getting handsome coaches arriving all the time?"

"Nowt to do with you. Come back Tuesday week at 7 in't mornin' and we'll see about whether you can work 'ere then."

With that, Arthur was dismissed.

Chapter 109

As Arthur walked away from the castle, he felt much more relaxed than he had on arrival. The head groomsman had seemed impressed by his knowledge of horses and that wasn't surprising as he had always enjoyed working with them. That was the first step. Who knew? He may even get to see the Scottish queen. What a pity that would be in his servile position, wearing servants' clothes. He must always make sure that he looked as smart as possible in case he should catch her eye. After all, it seemed he hadn't lost his ability to charm the ladies. But trying to charm a queen was a different matter. Particularly this queen whose feelings were mixed about being in this country, it appeared. He made sure he was standing out of sight of the magnificent coach he had seen arriving. Just as he had been hoping to see the coat of arms, the door had been opened and all he could see was a green satin interior, so beautiful that he no longer cared who the occupants were. He was so amazed by this coach that, by the time it started to be taken away, its occupants had disappeared into the castle. No matter. He wouldn't know them anyway. Well, not yet. He had been told to return to start his duties in the stables in two weeks' time. In the meantime, he would play dice and cards in the village. He must be careful, though, to ensure that he wasn't recognised, although that wasn't likely as, on his return to the inn, he would be transformed into the gentleman he was. For the moment, he had told the head groom that he was lodging with friends in the village. When he had asked who, as he might know them, Arthur had diverted his attention to one of the particularly fine horses. In any case, who knew, perhaps he would be able to stay at the castle in due course. The head groom had hinted that, provided he did his job well, that may be a possibility. He mustn't forget, though, that the main reason he was here in Castle Bolton was to enjoy tricking people out of their money as well as earning a little more at the castle's stables. Although he would never own such a place as Bolton Castle, he would see how such a magnificent dwelling was run. In that way, the newly-acquired manor he intended to purchase would be the envy of all who lived in these parts. They did speak in a way he hadn't heard before, though. He must teach himself to sound like them so that they would confide in him more readily. He didn't, after all, want to arouse suspicion.

Chapter 110

Margory felt nervous at the prospect of meeting the Scottish Queen, particularly as Bess had said that Sir William Cecil, when writing to her husband, had instructed that no-one was to visit Mary without permission. However, Bess had added that one of Cecil's subordinate colleagues had found reason to visit and, as the complaining queen had expressed such disappointment in her surroundings, Bess had deemed it beneficial to introduce a lady of her own faith who, she knew, would be of absolutely no threat to the English monarch and may result in Mary's feeling a little more relaxed. None of this, however, served to calm Margory's rattling nerves. Although she was the daughter of a Lord of the Manor, and in spite of the fact that the Countess of Shrewsbury was a good friend, this would be the first time she had met a queen. It had helped to alleviate her stress when Bess had suggested they buy new clothes for the visit and had advised Margory on just what would be appropriate. Margory hoped that her fashionable external presentation would hide her internal quaking.

The journey from Chatsworth had been very pleasant and Bess had continued to suggest how Margory should conduct herself in the queen's presence. So by the time they had arrived at Bolton Castle – which quite took Margory's breath away, with its high walls and splendid surroundings - she felt fairly comfortable in the knowledge that she would be in the presence of a queen who knew that, not only was she a friend of the Countess but, eventually, would also learn that they had the old faith in common. In fact, her tummy twinkled at the thought of being able to discuss openly what an important part her religion played in her life. This was something she had been unable to do for a very long time. Well, since her parents' death, really. Not only was Arthur disinterested in any religion whatsoever, it was well known that, when Elizabeth had ascended the throne, she had made it clear that she wished to unite the country under the Protestant umbrella. Although Margory had never met Queen Elizabeth, and in spite of the fact that Bess was a close friend of hers and extremely loyal to her, Margory was beginning to realise that, should any of her courtiers not be Protestant, provided they did not openly worship, she would look the other way. This, she knew to be true of her two favourite musicians, Byrd and Tallis, as well as Sir Gilbert Gerard, her Attorney General. Bess had made it clear to Margory that Queen Elizabeth was a very clever person whose political acumen was greatly admired. And Bess should know, for she had been at court many times. She had told her that the court was not a large one and that she had seen at first hand how cleverly Queen Elizabeth managed it. While Margory found it very interesting to hear detail of how the court was run, she could never, ever forget that, of course, it was due to Queen Elizabeth's spies, working secretly, that it had been discovered her parents were recusants. While she was very much looking forward to meeting Mary, Queen of Scots, she knew that she would never enjoy an audience with Queen Elizabeth in the same way, should the situation arise. How could she, knowing that she was responsible for the demise of her dear parents who had done nothing wrong, other than worship in the way they and their parents before them had worshipped. But such a meeting was not likely to happen anyway. Yes, her meeting with Queen Mary would be entirely different – that's if the Countess was able to arrange it, of course.

Chapter 111

"Countess. I am very surprised that you should think I could speak to anyone, irrespective of their faith, without the presence of my own ladies-in-waiting. You and I have met occasionally, of course, and I have enjoyed those meetings, coupled, as they are, with embroidery. Who do you say this lady is? Yes, I am aware that you know her well, but I know her not at all. How do I know that she is not here by the command of Queen Elizabeth to hear how I practise my Roman faith?"

"I am sure your Majesty realises…"

"Oh, I, too, am sure, Countess, that you mean well. However, I am also equally sure that your first loyalty is to your Queen, your husband, the Earl, and your country. No. Never have I been alone with anyone, and certainly not a stranger, whatever their faith. Do you not think that I have endured enough, both in Scotland and since coming to England? I no longer know who I can trust. I am moved around, I know not where, sometimes with all my court of 60 attendants, mainly with only some of those who serve me. Although I am told I am Queen Elizabeth's guest, I am fully aware that I am her prisoner, although she will never be heard to utter that word. Why? Because we are not only related but are both royal. Were she to mistreat me, it would reflect very badly on her own, royal status."

At that, the tall Queen stood, and the Countess, although much smaller, also rose to her feet.

"I am sure, Countess, that you do not wish to keep your friend – what did you say her name was? – ah yes, Mistress Margory Wright, waiting. And as you have quite a long drive, I suggest you leave now. I shall, of course, look forward to seeing you again, when we can resume our embroidery. I look forward to receiving your message. Of course, I know not how long I shall be at Tutbury Castle, but am sure you are far more familiar with where I shall be, when, than am I. Queen Elizabeth and your husband, of course, are making those arrangements, so I await their instructions."

As the Countess was about to remonstrate, she was interrupted.

"Yes, instructions is how I regard them, not decisions. After all, I am at the mercy of Elizabeth, as is your husband, the Earl."

Realising that she was being dismissed, Bess curtsied and left the room. No wonder her husband was going grey earlier than anticipated, she thought.

Chapter 112

Margory said nothing as she and Bess were handed into the coach. Her friend's face said it all. Clearly, the meeting with the Scottish Queen had not been played out as expected. Bess looked annoyed as she gazed out at the magnificent gardens and parks, leaving the castle to diminish as the horses galloped away strongly.

Touching her friend's hand lightly, she said,

"Please do not be stressed, Bess. I know not what happened in your audience with Queen Mary and I do not wish to know, unless you would like to tell me at some time. I have enjoyed seeing you again and I know that you had both the Scottish Queen's and my best interests at heart in suggesting what you did. But perhaps it is better that our common faith should not have been discussed between the two of us, alone. Secrecy veiling such an important matter was never going to be easy to arrange. And who knows? The walls of Bolton Castle may have ears and that information overheard may have been passed to those who wish Queen Mary ill. However diplomatically our Queen Elizabeth steps, and although she and I do not share the same faith, I wish her no ill, as I know, certainly, neither do you. So I hope that you will put this meeting behind you and let us enjoy the rest of my visit to you so that we shall be in a position to look forward to our next meeting."

"Thank you, my dear, for your understanding. I am, indeed, not only a little angry, but also disappointed that Queen Mary did not realise I was attempting to make her stay at our Bolton Castle a little more contented than I know it to be at the moment. You are quite right. I shall put the matter aside and try not to dwell on it further. I am particularly pleased, too, that my husband, the Earl, is unaware of our intended mission today. Although he is very honoured indeed to have been asked by Queen Elizabeth to be in charge of accommodating Queen Mary in several of our castles, I know that it is not proving to be an easy task. And, indeed, it is also an expensive one. But I shall not burden you with any further information about that. As you say, once back at Chatsworth, let us enjoy the rest of your stay. I shall ask my children to join us once more, so that they can tell us about everything they've been doing."

This was the first time that Margory had seen her friend annoyed about anything and she felt sorry that she was a part of the reason for that displeasure. Queen Mary's presence in England was clearly not easy for the Countess and her husband as they did all they could to help Queen Elizabeth. As it hadn't been possible for her to meet the Scottish Queen, she would pray that she remained safe and happy in England, even though it may not be easy for either her nor those asked to make her comfortable. In the meantime, she would enjoy the rest of her stay with Bess and her children before returning to The Manor. It had now been some time since she had seen Arthur. She really must try to please him more on his return.

Chapter 113

Arthur walked slowly back to where he had left his horse. It was only due to the fact that there was no-one to be seen for miles that he had taken the risk of leaving it here. He was so lost in his thoughts that he barely noticed the beautiful, wide open countryside of lush grassland and thick woodland. This was serving his purpose better than he could have hoped. Bolton and the Olde Man & Scythe were several days' ride from Bolton Castle. That lack of proximity would serve his purpose well. When in Bolton, he would play his gentleman, Lord of the Manor role, dressing, speaking and spending accordingly. While he would continue to stay at that inn and make money by playing dice and cards as well as learning chess there, he would travel in style to other such inns in the area and pursue his game-playing there. In that way, he wouldn't become very well known at any of these locations, neither would he tell where he was staying. It was to his advantage that fine inns were few and far between in this area. It would also mean that no-one would realise that his game of dice was being played differently from theirs. By only visiting these inns occasionally, there was little likelihood of his game strategy becoming known. On the other hand, he could take to one of his horses and travel to Bolton Castle in order to get to know the ways of the castle and when Sir Francis was there. That would mean that when the Scottish Queen was moved, perhaps to Tutbury Castle, he would be well informed as to when this would happen. By then, he would also know her stables and all the servants well so that he could, one day, when the time was right, become the gentleman he was in order to request an audience with Sir Francis.

As Arthur mounted his horse, he felt more satisfied than he had for quite some time. He now had a plan that he was sure would facilitate his becoming a rich landowner in this part of England. For the time being, he would remain here as, returning to Hertfordshire, even for a short time, would weaken his plan. On the one hand, by visiting different inns in the Bolton area, he would not become known very well. On the other hand, in the guise of a servant, he would get to know the procedures and staff of a castle at Bolton Castle. They would, after all, be superior to the ways of a manor house in which he had worked all those years ago. What was more, if his wife became intimate with Hugh whatever-his-name-was in his absence, that could only be to his advantage. Her punishment would, of course, be his taking her against her will once again. Under the circumstances, any man in his position would totally understand that action. Yes, this plan of his with its three parts was beginning to unfold in a highly satisfactory way.

Second thoughts. In order to put his plan into action properly, he would definitely need to remain in these parts for quite some time, so it would be wiser to return to Hertfordshire now. After all, he would be planting a second seed in Margory and he was not interested in being at The Manor during its growth. It was always so boring to see a woman growing fat and listless. He had seen that with Lucy. He would return to the inn at Bolton, leave his belongings there and take his coach to Hertfordshire. Who knew? Perhaps he would interrupt his wife's relationship with that man, Hugh. Or maybe she would be away from The Manor once again, visiting who knew whom. He cared not. That is what he would do.

Chapter 114

"My dear Margory, I am so very pleased to see you and looking very well."

As she stepped out of the coach, Margory experienced a rush of opposing emotional bubbles at the totally unexpected sight of Hugh. For the first time, she recognised and capitulated to a feeling of utter love for him. At the same time, she knew – as she always had – that that love could never be requited. How easy it would be, she thought, to simply give in to those feelings and allow herself to be embraced and enfolded in their mutual love. Instead, she felt rather foolish simply standing, looking at him.

"Is anything wrong, Margory? You seem a little distant. Can I help with anything?"

Margory continued to stand, simply gazing at this lovely man. How could she even begin to explain all the complexities she had experienced for such a long time?

It had not only been some time since she had seen Hugh, but also Arthur. But she cared not either where Arthur was, nor with whom. She now knew him so very well. As all he wished for her was hurt, inflicted, not only directly, as he had shown when insisting on entering her body by force but when, even worse, he had given so much pain to their baby. That, she would never forgive, and indeed, she would deprive herself of the wonderful love of her son in order to deprive Arthur of his satisfaction. But some of his actions must be her own fault, were they not? Perhaps so, but that did not mean she would risk her husband's infliction of pain upon such an innocent. If pain had to be inflicted, it would be to herself, the child's mother. But how could she explain all this to this upright, totally moral and just man standing before her? How could he understand such difficulties that were totally alien to his natural character? Margory just didn't know how she could stand outside The Manor which her parents and grandparents had owned, on this delightfully sunny day, and begin trying to explain a situation which, she was sure, he could not start to comprehend when it was so very different from his own?

"Thank you so much for asking, Hugh. I have just returned from an interesting visit to my friend, the Countess of Shrewsbury. I'm so very sorry, but, as I have been away, I must speak to Goodwife Sykes right away to make sure that all is well here. Excuse me, Hugh."

It pained Margory so much to see Hugh's disappointment, coupled with a puzzled expression. Once again, she longed to embrace him and tell him that he was the most wonderful person she had ever met. Instead, she had to endure his turning away, shoulders slumped. How could she bear it? But bear it she must. As Hugh mounted his horse and prepared to depart, he glanced over his shoulder, "I shall not trouble you again, Margory, unless I receive a message from you to say that I can be of help."

She thought her heart would break.

Chapter 115

"My dear mistress Margory, what ails you? I have never seen such a very sad face. Are you ill?"

For the first time ever, Margory spoke sharply to this good woman who she had known all her life.

"Ask Lucy or someone to unpack my chest. I shall retire to my bedchamber as I suddenly feel extremely tired. Tell cook I shall not be needing any supper and shall rest until the morning."

Margory immediately felt so very sorry for speaking in such a way to this loyal, elderly and increasingly infirm member of her staff. She must make it up to her the following day. But first, she could not wait to rest her head.

***

Margory lay in bed, on her back, gazing up at the beautiful plasterwork ceiling. In spite of her utter exhaustion, she felt wide awake and very sad. That was the first time she had ever spoken unkindly to, not only Hugh but Goodwife Sykes. Goodwife Sykes who, over so many years, had been loyalty itself. Goodwife Sykes who was now elderly and not in the best of health. Not only that, she had dismissed dear, dear Hugh in an unforgiveable way. She had sent away the man she cared for deeply. His look of surprise and disappointment smote her as surely as any sword. How could she have done that?

Lying there, Margory thought about the circumstances that had brought her to this sorry state; perhaps it wasn't so surprising after all. Her devoted parents had been put to death. Arthur had then returned and given her the news of his fraud. But in spite of all that, Goodwife Sykes and the rest of The Manor's household had stood by her side. Also, her parents' good friends in Brockminster had been the very kind instruments of her return to bringing babies into this world. But that skill had been misread by envy so that gossip had accused her of witchcraft. In the midst of all that, of course, she had met Hugh who had worked hard in returning The Manor to its former glory. Although that friendship was pure, it had gradually grown. But then, of course, Arthur, penurious Arthur, had returned, as he always did when he no longer had money for the lifestyle he wished to pursue. And that return had produced Henry. She did not intend to dwell on the means by which her child had been produced, but produced he had been. And, from the very moment of his birth, he had been the star of her life. The star that shone ever more brightly as he grew. How very much she missed him. Again, she would not dwell on thoughts so painful that she could not bear to think about them. Henry was safe. Henry was well. She thanked the Lord for her friend, Marion's intervention at a time when she knew not how she could continue to witness his ill treatment by Arthur. Would Henry forget her? This thought was so unbearable that, once again, she put it aside. She was convinced that it was for absolutely the right reasons that Henry no longer lived at The Manor. Not for the moment anyway.

Then there was her growing friendship with Bess, the Countess of Shrewsbury who, herself, had not had an easy life, of course, entering it, at an early age as she had, as a Ward of Court – just one of the ways the Crown replenished its treasury and had done so since medieval times when it was necessary to raise an army quickly and inexpensively. Why did wars have to be such an omnipresent part of life, wondered Margory? Why couldn't people live in peace with each other? That was as difficult a question as her wonderings about why everyone couldn't accept each other's different ways of worship. Why did she have to praise the Lord in secret? But enough of that thought. She had promised her father that that was what she would do – and she had. It was probably just as well that Bess's kind thought of sharing her faith with the Scottish Queen had come to nought. Margory was so very fortunate to have Bess as a friend. Yes. Marion, Bess and Hugh were her pieces of gold that enriched her life, with Henry her sparkling gem who she would love, whatever happened to her. Were it not for him, Margory was not sure she would have a strong reason to continue living. But that was against everything she had ever been taught. God did not forgive those who gave up hope. Wasn't Judas an example of that? After his betrayal of Christ and seeing the result, he had hanged himself. No, she mustn't stop hoping that, one day, she and Henry would live under the same roof. What a beautiful thought that was. As for sharing her love with Hugh, that could never be, so she would not dwell on it. No, she must try very hard to, perhaps, like Arthur. Margory's reflections stopped there. Was that possible? Had her heart closed entirely against him?

Chapter 116

Arthur stepped down from the coach. How dare there be no-one there to receive the Lord of the Manor? The place was quieter than he had ever known. He could hear the birds singing. Not that their noise interested him at all. He could hear the workers in the fields. That sound took him back to his childhood and early years before he had met the plain woman he had been persuaded to marry. Where was everybody?

Arthur strode into the vast hall and looked around. No-one in sight. He really must punish his wife for neglecting her duties. After all, the least a Lord of the Manor could expect would be a greeting on his return, even if only by servants. This must be his wife's doing. Once again, she was not managing the household of which he was master. At least that old hag of a Head Housekeeper, Sykes, was always around to be of service. Yes, he would have liked all his guests to be greeted by pretty, young servants. But Margory had insisted that her previous servants were retained. What a foolish woman she was. Why would any Lord of the Manor wish to look upon elderly women, day in, day out?

Arthur banged the floor with his cane. Nothing. He banged again. Harder. At that, Goodwife Sykes limped into his presence.

"Ah, so my manor is not totally bereft of servants."

"I do beg your pardon, your Lordship. I don't think we were aware of your return."

"And why, may I ask, should I report my every movement to anyone? Are you suggesting that you and my other servants should know when I come and when I go?" Arthur walked up to the housekeeper and stood so close that she could see his nostrils flaring. It reminded her of a horse's flaring; at the thought, a small smile escaped.

"How dare you laugh at me! How dare you! What, may I ask, is so amusing that you smile in the face of your Lord and master?" At that, Arthur raised his hand.

"Your Lordship. How good it is to see you again."

Arthur looked over the shoulder of the diminutive, now shaking housekeeper.

"Lucy. Well, I'm glad to see that someone here knows how to behave when the Lord of the Manor returns. But no sign of my dear wife, Margory. Has she left the Manor once again? Where, may I ask, is she?" Regaining her composure, Goodwife Sykes replied,

"Her Ladyship has retired to her bedchamber."

"What! It is only 3 of the clock. Is she alone?" Once again, Arthur stepped forward so that he was only inches away from the housekeeper.

Goodwife Sykes and Lucy gasped. Attempting to retain her composure with this man for whom she had little liking, the housekeeper straightened her shoulders.

"Her Ladyship was weary on her return from Chatsworth, your Lordship, and retired to her bedchamber, asking that we do not disturb her until the morning."

Pushing past the two women so hard that they both almost lost their balance, Arthur flew up the stairs, two at a time. Gazing after him, they heard his banging of the bedchamber door which closed on their knowing what happened next.

Chapter 117

Margory was just beginning to drift into dreamland when the slamming of the bedchamber door drew her upright as though she was joined to it by cord. Her husband stood before her, hands on hips.

"Well, now I know why my manor is so disorganised. Now I know why there is no-one to greet me on my return and perform the duties I am due as Lord of the Manor. Now I know because I return unexpectedly to find my wife in our bed in the middle of the afternoon. Tell me, dearest wife, did you retire alone or have you, once more, been keeping company with your Brockminster friend? You have clearly been brought up to be very lazy. Even Lucy, who bore my children, and who did not have the wealthy childhood that you enjoyed, was not to be found in bed in the middle of the afternoon. Once again, you must be punished."

The ears at the bedchamber door rushed away on hearing the scream. This was clearly a repeat of the sounds they had heard three years before that had culminated in the birth of Henry. Surely the Lord of the Manor was not taking his wife by force? Did the mistress dislike her husband so much that she could not lay with him? Would this result, once again, in the mistress being very ill for the next nine months? So many questions being whispered by so many servants. Goodwife Sykes usually stopped any gossip before it got underway. But on this occasion, she sat quietly and listened. How fortunate they had almost all worked for Mistress Margory's parents whose relationship had been based on love and respect, in spite of their perhaps, occasionally, not agreeing on everything. After all, that was usual, wasn't it? Also, as they all knew, the master of the house, while listening to his wife's opinion, always made the final decision on the way forward. But force and bullying had never been a part of their relationship. How had the manor's master and mistress come to this? That scream was not one of pleasure, but of pain. How could her mistress continue to accept being treated so badly? It certainly appeared that that was what she intended to do. The elderly servant put her head on her arms on the table and fell into a troubled sleep. The hushed whisperings began again.

Chapter 118

That was enough. This time, Margory did not intend to be forced into doing anything she did not want to do. Also, she did not wish to bear a second child by this man – should that be the outcome. Oh, she would never forget that, had it not been for her persuading Arthur to marry her, she would not be in this awful position. But did God intend her to continue in a relationship that did not have love on either side? After all, love was the most important thing in this world. She knew that, without a doubt. And this was not love.

Margory kicked and screamed. Suddenly, she felt different, more determined. This may be her husband but, not only did he not like her, she didn't like him either, however much she tried. She realised that Arthur had never loved her. All she had ever wished for was a husband who loved her, whom she loved and for a family to grow from that love. Of course, she accepted that she had made a mistake all those years ago, but hadn't he acquiesced to that error.

Kick! Scream!

"Oh, I do like this part of you, dear wife. Perhaps…"

"Do you like this?" Finally, gathering all her strength, Margory kicked Arthur in the private part of his body that was one of the roots of his evil. A part that was much lower than his laughing face. And again. And again. Oh, that clearly hurt him – a lot. So, gathering all the strength she could muster, she kicked that area one final time. This time, Arthur quickly curled, cat-like, moaning. Immediately, Margory dressed and fled, knowing not where. All she did know was that she had to leave her home because, if she didn't, Arthur would come after her. Running to the stables, she jumped on the nearest horse and flew.

Chapter 119

Margory rode as she had never ridden before. Mile after mile, field after field. Long hair streaming behind her. She was fire fuelled by fear. So many thoughts jangled while she rode. Arthur would kill her, she knew, were he to find her. But why was she not feeling utter grief at leaving her childhood home? Why? Because she was going home. Home to the roof that housed the love of her dear son. Home to her loyal friend, Marion. She did not allow herself to think further about the place to which she was fleeing. When flying from The Manor, she had thought she did not know where she was going. But of course, she did. She was re-entering the world of love while leaving behind her childhood home, the door of which was certainly closed to her.

***

Arthur lay there. He hurt in a place he had never felt hurt before. The pain had been excruciating. He had felt pain like no other, ever. This woman would suffer. He knew not how, he knew not when. But she would suffer. And he would also bring down those who called themselves friends of hers. But first, he must recover and resume his dignity. Had he heard whisperings and even covert laughter when in the midst of his pain? They would wish they hadn't whispered. They would wish they hadn't giggled. Stupid women.

It was now even more important that he established himself among those who thought themselves to be higher and mightier than others. He was, after all, building his riches in another part of England. Knowing the rich was so important. He knew the Countess of Shrewsbury, although he was disappointed that he had not yet met the Earl. He was planning to meet Sir Francis Knollys. Who knew? Perhaps he may even meet the Queen of Scots. She was, after all, purported to be contacting overseas friends who may put her on the English throne. What did he care about religion, be it Queen Elizabeth's Protestantism or Mary's Catholicism? Perhaps he could use one or the other to further his own ends. After all, Sir Francis Knollys and the Earl of Shrewsbury were both at Queen Elizabeth's court frequently. How would his devout Catholic wife feel then? Oh yes, when they had been intimate all those years ago, she had shared with him her secret place of worship. He was sure that she would still worship there, the place in the library at The Manor. By the time he had finished with her, she would wish she had never been born. Just his word in Protestant ears would walk his wife down the path to the gallows. Her parents had been recusants and so was she. She had escaped punishment for her secrecy once. No more.

Chapter 120

Arthur left hurriedly, in the opposite direction from his wife. He ordered the best carriage his wife's family had bought and took her jewels which included those of her mother. The jewels wouldn't be recognised in the other part of the country and they would bring him nearer to his goal of buying another manor house in the North West. He had also decided to take more clothes from The Manor, both smart and not-so-smart.

"Olde Man and the Scythe, Bolton. As quick as you can."

Arthur sat back, trying to gain a comfortable position. He was still in agony. Once in Bolton, he would rest awhile before putting his plan into action. He certainly didn't intend to return to The Manor for some considerable time. How dare she, a mere woman, do that to him, her husband? He would never forget how she had behaved; he would make sure she didn't forget her actions either.

Gradually feeling a little more comfortable, he sat back. Now was the time to put his plan into action; playing games to make money around several inns in the middle of the country and north-west. He would ensure that it became known he was Lord of the Manor in Hertfordshire, with the intention of purchasing a property further north. Also, by moving around, his gaming technique would not become known to those he saw only occasionally. At the same time, he would tend the horses of the Earl of Shrewsbury, first at Bolton Castle, then Tutbury and who knew where after that. He'd heard tell of Sheffield Castle being a possible place for the Scottish queen to stay. In that way he would increase his income while following where she was going. He would also get to know what Sir Francis and the Earl looked like so that, should he encounter them while playing games as a gentleman, while they wouldn't know him, he would know them. That would put him in the advantageous position of knowing when he could arrange a loan. After the way his wife had treated him, he may not return to Hertfordshire at all. On the other hand, he would definitely now consider selling The Manor in Greenwillows which would expedite his northern purchase. No, whatever happened, he would not return there for quite some time.

Chapter 121

"Margory, Margory, whatever is wrong? My dear friend, you look as though you've been riding for days. And those clothes – your hair. My dear. Come on in. Abner, I know you were about to go out, so I suggest you do that so that Margory can tell me what ails her. Are you able, on this one occasion, to take Henry and Jacob with you? I need to speak to Margory so that I can see what is wrong as she is so clearly very upset. Thank you."

Giving her husband a swift kiss on the cheek, she re-entered the cottage and sat next to her friend. But as soon as Marion put her arms around her, Margory burst into tears.

"My dearest friend. I don't think I've seen you as upset as this since your trial. Sit and rest and I shall get a small ale for both of us."

Margory leaned back in the chair and closed her eyes. Finally, she didn't intend to accept Arthur's boorish behaviour any longer. But that was easier said than done. What was she to do now? Where would she go and where would she live? As she never knew when her husband was returning to The Manor, she didn't intend to take up residence there at the moment. She really did feel that her life was in danger, should Arthur return. Not only had she given him severe pain physically, she had kicked his manhood. She knew he would never forgive her. Not that she wanted his forgiveness. However, she needed to consider what he would do next. Would he now put his plan into action of committing her to a mental institution? Was he still at The Manor? Margory had never known what Arthur did in the North West of England – other than when he had called upon her friend, Bess, unexpectedly. And no-one had known that, other than Arthur. Had it not been for the fact that Bess was such a good friend and followed up

Arthur's visit by a message, she wouldn't have known about it, either.

"Marion, I need to speak to you more urgently, probably, than I have ever spoken to you before."

Taking a seat next to Margory, and handing her the small ale, Marion waited for her friend to tell her what was wrong. No sooner had she finished telling her what had happened, Margory couldn't believe her ears. Marion was actually laughing. Out loud! Uncontrollably. On and on.

"Marion. Did you hear what I said? I kicked Arthur in a place that clearly gave him a great deal of pain. In fact, I kicked him several times."

"In the same place?"

"Yes. As I didn't intend to submit to his forcing his body into mine yet again – in spite of the fact that the previous result was my beloved Henry – and as I was clearly placing my kick in a part of Arthur's body that pained him a great deal, I continued to do it. I have never known that that particular part of a man's body would hurt so much when kicked. How would I?"

Marion was still having difficulty reigning in her laughter, but when her friend continued to look in puzzlement at her mirth, she drew breath and tried to stop. Patting her skirt, she tried very hard to contain her laughter.

"My dear, innocent friend. As you are an only child, an only daughter, it doesn't surprise me that you are not very familiar with certain parts of a man's body that would give great pain. I suspect, too, that you have not come across the word 'rape' either. Because that is what Arthur did to you three years ago. And that is what he has now tried to do yet again. Your action, as you saw, stopped him very effectively in continuing with his second attempt. And, do you know, Margory, I don't think he will try that again – ever! Now, what we must ensure is that he doesn't try to harm you.

Because that is certainly going to be something he will try to do. This is what I suggest."

Sipping her small ale and beginning to feel a little more relaxed, Margory listened to what her friend said.

"When Abner returns, I shall tell him of your ordeal and my suggestion as to how we deal with it, if that meets with your approval."

Margory felt bereft of all her decision-making skills. However, she did have one, very important question to ask.

"What about Henry and Jacob? Where will they go and who will take care of them while we're away, Marion?"

"I know exactly who I shall ask. Not only that, I am absolutely sure that they will be received with open, loving arms. Once again, as before, Margory, it will be better if you do not know what I have in mind for Henry's care as Arthur will undoubtedly want to hurt you as much as possible. And, of course, he is well aware that he gives you a great deal of suffering when hurting Henry."

Knowing that Marion would be arranging for Henry's safe-keeping was music to Margory's ears. While, of course, she wanted to hear Marion's plans for her son, she realised that it was better for her not to have that knowledge. And, as always, she trusted her friend's judgement totally. Marion continued,

"As soon as we are all ready, we shall go to The Manor so that you can bathe and dress, as well as gathering together everything you need."

"Oh, Marion, I've just recalled something. An item that Arthur carries everywhere with him. This needs to be taken into account by Abner."

"Well done in remembering that, Margory, it is certainly of great importance. I shall tell Abner what you have said."

Chapter 122

Marion then left, telling Margory to rest, and she would return soon.

Feeling a little better, Margory was, nevertheless, shocked, on Marion's return, to see that she was not only accompanied by Abner, but also by Hugh.

Pre-empting Margory's query as to why Hugh should accompany them, she said,

"Don't worry, Margory. I think the time has come for everyone to realise what a very good friend to you Hugh is. It is only Arthur's nastiness – and perhaps his desire, so that his treatment of you would be justified – that assumes you and he are more than friends. We know the truth of your relationship and this is not the time to play games. The truth must prevail. I have a further suggestion which is that, when we arrive at The Manor, you send a message to your friend, the Countess, asking if we may stay with her for the moment and that you will tell her why on our arrival."

Margory nodded. Yes, that would also guarantee her safety and that of her friends. How wonderful to have such good friends at any time, but particularly now. She smiled at Marion.

"That's better, my dear. Right. Are you ready to leave for The Manor now? We have received the loan of a very good coach and horses so that our journey to Chatsworth will be as comfortable as possible."

Was there anything Marion had not thought of?

Chapter 123

Abner and Hugh remained in the coach on arrival at The Manor, as some of the servants may have been unaware of Margory's friendships, particularly with Hugh, so may have misinterpreted his presence. Margory was all too aware of infectious gossip, even in her own household.

"Goodwife Sykes. My friends and I are going to visit the Countess of Shrewsbury once again, and, this time, I would like you to accompany me, with some of my own personal servants. In that way, I shall know that you are resting when you need to rest. But also, I would value your accompanying my servants who do not have your experience. In this way, they can benefit from knowing procedures in an aristocratic household, while being of practical help. Also, as I am unsure as to when my husband will return to The Manor, I do not wish to put you in the difficult position of needing to tell him that you do not know when my return will be. You are very precious to me, Goodwife Sykes, and I shall not risk exposing you to difficulties that are not of your making."

"Under the circumstances, I think it will be appropriate for Lucy to manage the household at The Manor. As I have previously mentioned, she was, of course, in charge of my husband's servants in another part of the country when he lived there with her and their children for several years. So I think she will learn a great deal by handling this situation that I find myself in, now. Please ask Lucy to stop what she is doing and come to the library now. I know your soft heart, Goodwife Sykes, but do not take 'no' for an answer. I wish to see her immediately. If necessary, please remind her that this is my family's Manor House. But I am sure you will not need to do that as you are so very capable in dealing with the servants. I shall go to the stables to speak to

Thomas and inform him that he is in charge of the estate. I understand that my husband has left him in charge previously."

Chapter 124

1570

Although still feeling rather shaky, Margory felt that this may be the beginning of a new life. A positive life. One with more love in it than she had experienced until now. Of course, the only person missing was Henry. But his absence was due to a very good reason. She knew that he was safe and well and that was what mattered to her. Unlike the Countess of Shrewsbury, who had several children, she had only the one. So her love was not divided. Her heart was so full of love for Henry that she knew not, in any case, how there could be room for the love of any other children.

Abner had given instructions to both coachmen that, although they should proceed quickly, the journey was to be taken with care. He had made it clear that treasured people were travelling.

Margory felt that she was enclosed in a blanket of love, travelling to, not only a good friend, but a friend who was wise and influential. She was looking forward to speaking to Bess in confidence once again, this time, in the company of Marion whom Bess had met already, of course. Indeed, she had also met Abner and Hugh which meant that this visit would be one based on a flowering friendship of all those present. Margory was beginning to feel increasingly content.

"Are you all right, my dear?" Marion leaned over and put her hand on Margory's.

"Yes, thanks to you and your sensible suggestions, made so much easier by your accompanying me with Abner to Chatsworth."

Even now, Margory found it difficult to include Hugh, even in conversation. But there he was, looking as kind as always. She hadn't realised how sensitive he was, too, to her feelings. Although she knew he was aware of how she felt about him, he nevertheless sat as far away as he could from her in the coach. Neither did he speak directly to her, but addressed Marion and Abner about topics of little importance. She did notice, however, that he glanced at her periodically and, in doing so, his face reflected her feelings. This was the closest she had sat to him, even during his days of caring for The Manor. She was constantly learning more about him, and she loved that.

Chapter 125

Finally, Arthur's coach arrived at the inn in Bolton and he jumped out, ordering the manservant to carry in his belongings.

Bounding up to his room, he changed into a finer ruff, hose, doublet and leather breeches. He then combed his hair before putting on a tall hat. His wife had bought a mirror for The Manor, of course, at great cost, which annoyed him. He must watch out for a small mirror so that he could check on just how smart he was looking when travelling. He knew that important people would have them. Perhaps he could visit Chatsworth again unannounced and take a look there. The Countess was wealthy, after all, and wouldn't miss a small mirror. But for now he knew that he looked smart enough. After all, at the moment, his main occupation – in addition to gaining as much money as possible when playing dice – would be watching and listening for Sir Francis Knollys. His journey to the Hertfordshire manor had been a waste of time, he was already established there. This was where he needed to be known.

"Good day, my man. And with whom can I expect to play dice today in your fine establishment?"

"I don't believe you have met the players seated at the table over there, sir, have you? While you are joining them, I shall fetch a bottle of your favourite claret from the cellar."

This was more like it. He was not only becoming known, but to be known as a gentleman of fine taste. Arthur puffed his chest with pride.

"May I join you? I don't believe we have met. My manor house is in Hertfordshire but I intend to spend an increasing amount of time in this part of the world as I wish to purchase a manor house here, too. May I offer you a glass of claret? Let us begin."

Arthur thought that the men appeared to be servants, but well dressed servants. He would allow himself to be seen playing along with them. After all, they would have no idea how he played dice. Tomorrow, he would journey to another inn and do the same thing. It really was so easy to deceive these sorts of people. He stroked his chin as though contemplating his next throw. Two hours and three bottles of claret later, with Arthur generously re-filling the glasses of his companions while drinking much less himself, the men wished him a good evening and staggered out of the inn. How easy it was to deceive, thought Arthur. By ensuring that he played these games at several inns, quite some distance apart, he could maximise his earnings while ensuring that no-one got to know the way he played very well.

The following two weeks proved to be very lucrative for Arthur. It was fortunate, he thought, that he had recently purchased a larger leather purse attached to his belt. He made sure that no-one ever saw just where he kept it. Although he continued to carry protection with him at all times, it would be foolish of him to allow his fellow players to see where he deposited the coins. Oh, he had noticed a few of his companions take a quick look to see where he was putting them, but by then he had gathered so many that he cared not. He was fortunate not to have met a wild rogue in his travels and, if he did, he would not indicate to them where he kept his purse, either, of course. Common thievery was rife everywhere and Arthur knew that these people begged and, when asking for coin, should he show a quick response, the person would immediately know that he had disposable wealth in his purse. As the word 'thief' crossed his mind, Arthur hesitated. But only for a moment. His game playing was not thievery. He used a skill that his fellow players did not have. That was quite different. He brushed away the thought. He and others in these parts knew him for the person he was: an increasingly wealthy gentleman who already owned a manor house and was about to own another. However, Arthur also knew that the timing of the playing-out of his two roles, those of gentleman and servant, was crucial. Feeling pleased with his earnings gained in game playing so far, now was the time to return to Bolton Castle. Indeed, he had heard that the Scottish queen was to be moved to Tutbury very soon, and even then to Sheffield Castle as Tutbury was little more than a hunting lodge. By the time she went to Tutbury, Arthur would be known by the other servants and would have become one of them. He would be included in any chatter and, with Mary in their midst, gossip would be everywhere. How useful it was that many enjoyed talking about other people's lives.

Chapter 126

Arthur was quite right in his assumption of increasing gossip at Queen Mary's court. It was said that Queen Elizabeth's treatment of her was not the best; also, the Earl's allowance from Elizabeth was woefully poor. Not only that, part of the financial difficulty was the fact that, whenever someone from Scotland was anywhere near, they joined the royal household. So while it was clear to everyone that their Queen Mary's allowance was not sufficient, their numbers were increasing, which lowered it even further.

It was this tittle-tattle that greeted Arthur's delighted ears on his return to the stables at Bolton Castle. It couldn't have suited him better. While the queen and those close to her were totally preoccupied with the conditions in which they lived and her growing number of servants which she could not afford, it was so much easier for Arthur to slide in and become yet another number. He would do more listening then talking. He discovered, too, that Queen Mary was about to move to Tutbury Castle.

Having ensured that he was known to be one of the stable hands, he returned to his life of dice playing.

Chapter 127

The Countess received Margory and her friends with her usual alacrity.

"How very nice it is to see you all once again – Marion, Abner and Hugh." Then, taking Margory aside, gently,

"Do I take it it was considered beneficial for Henry not to be a part of this visit? I certainly do not wish to upset you, my dear, but I know how very much he means to you, hence my asking."

"I can't begin to tell you how much the judgement of my long-standing friend, Marion, means to me, Bess. I trust her implicitly and, on this occasion, she has made arrangements for both Henry and her own son, Jacob, to be cared for in our absence. Being the sensible person she is, she has not told me what those arrangements are, and it is better that I do not ask. But what I do know is that I trust Marion totally and whatever her arrangements are, I know that Henry will be safe. I care not how my husband treats me – although I shall speak to you about what has happened most recently – but I shall never again risk Henry's being treated in the way Arthur treated him."

Bess shook her head,

"It is, indeed, an evil adult who treats a babe in the way Arthur did. I know of no other who would do that. But you say that you have something more to tell me. As I assume that Marion knows what that will be, I suggest that the three of us take tea while the gentlemen walk in the grounds. I shall ask one of my housekeepers to show your trusted servants to their rooms. I think it will then be helpful for them to know where they will be working, after they have taken refreshment in the kitchens and rested."

"Thank you, Bess. I told my main housekeeper, Goodwife Sykes, in particular to accompany me as, not only is she elderly, but her health is not as good as I would like. Also, as my husband returns to The Manor when and if he wishes, and does not treat Goodwife Sykes, in particular, very well, I am unwilling to allow that to continue. Additionally, I suggested that the three other servants accompanied us as I know that I can leave Goodwife Sykes to arrange their duties, together with your own staff. At the same time, they will benefit from experiencing how an exceptionally well-run household such as yours is organised. In my absence, I have left someone in charge of The Manor who has had similar experience, running a manor house."

As it was clear that her friend would not be elaborating on who had been left in charge of the Hertfordshire manor, the Countess enquired no further.

Marion, Margory and Bess then retired to one of the drawing rooms where they had tea. There, Margory described her latest experience with Arthur, without saying what had happened in detail. The Countess listened intently and, what Margory did not describe fully, Bess's diplomatic intelligence filled in the gaps, her increasingly shocked face displaying all. Once again, Marion found it difficult to hide her mirth and, when Margory had finished, Bess sat back and clapped before going to her friend and giving her a hug.

"Very, very well done, Margory. You have no idea how delighted and proud I am to hear that you have finally resisted the actions of that bullying husband. Bullies are, after all, cowards. I am sure the shock of your actions was as great as the physical pain he felt. I also think you have been wise in bringing some of your own servants who may bear the brunt of his wrath, were he to return while you're away. I'm pleased that you have not taken that risk and I know that my own servants will make yours feel welcome at Chatsworth. Tomorrow, I have further news about Queen Mary's stay in this country. This time, it may be easier for you and her to speak, Margory. I shall tell you about it then. In the meantime, enjoy your walk with Hugh."

If Margory had felt any reservations about her behaviour towards Arthur which had been totally spontaneous and not at all premeditated, she was now reassured by, not only Marion, but the Countess. That relief met her pleasure in seeing Abner and Hugh walking in to join them. Could she now allow her feelings for Hugh to show, even if only a little? As though reading her mind, and echoing her suggestion made during their Christmas stay at Chatsworth, Bess said,

"Margory. Why don't you continue to show Hugh the gardens which will leave Marion and Abner to rest in their bed chamber."

Margory thought that her close friends were beginning to get to know her very well indeed and, on glancing at Hugh and noting his look of pleasure, she smiled as he drew her arm through his. That was to be the first of many such walks. Margory wondered how one man could be so wicked while another was so good. She put aside the thought. She would enjoy the company of the one who was so good in spite of the fact that, deep down, she did feel a slight guilt. For the first time in her life, she decided to ignore it.

"Come Margory. Abner and I have spent a very pleasant time looking at some of the gardens. But you know them a great deal better than either of us so we shall go wherever it pleases you."

At the touch of Hugh's arm and the sound of his kind voice, Margory felt something she had never felt before, in all of her 29 years. Had she been asked to describe it, she would have struggled, such was its newness. The closest she could come was to think that she felt love so strongly at that moment, she was quite overwhelmed, to the point of tears. It was as though that love had lain dormant and was now opening its petals, to the point of requesting permission to make its presence felt.

"Are you all right, Margory? Have I said something to upset you?" Hugh stopped and, turning Margory to face him, he kissed the wetness from both cheeks. That gesture was almost too much for Margory to bear.

"Quite the opposite, Hugh. Now let us continue to walk before I break down entirely. No. Please do not ask. All I shall say is that I wish this walk would never end."

Chapter 128

"That's him! That's him! That's the man who calls himself a gentleman while moving from one inn to another, cheating at dice."

There was no time for Arthur to collect his belongings. He ran from the inn around to the stables.

"Get the horses ready for me to take my coach now. Immediately." Pressing coins into the man's hand and indicating to the coach driver to leave, Arthur lay on the seat so that, should anyone glance inside, they would think the fast-moving coach was empty.

As they raced past the front of the inn, Arthur heard the inn keeper shouting, "And you haven't paid for your room here either. Don't ever come this way again unless you have payment in your hand. At the same time, you will face the consequences of your cheating."

Arthur lay there, still as a slug. He rapidly considered what his next move would be and where he should go next. Yes, that was it, he would go straight to Chatsworth. He hadn't given prior notice when he visited before – he would do the same again. Hopefully, this time, the Earl would be there and he would ask for a loan. Knocking on the coach roof.

"Driver. Stop at the best inn you can find between here and Chatsworth. I shall need to buy more suitable clothes before continuing my journey."

After a slight pause,

"Take me to The Seven Stars in Manchester. And make it fast."

"Yes, your Lordship." Knowing the Lord of the Manor as he did, the driver didn't query his instructions but increased the horses' speed to this newly requested destination.

Arthur was pleased to have recalled The Seven Stars which he already knew a little. He would receive the welcome he deserved as he had never played any games there. Also, Manchester was a large enough town that he could buy whatever he needed. He settled back, pleased to have thought of it. He would also look for a gift for the Countess of Shrewsbury. If the Earl was once again not there, he would need to speak to her. What a nuisance. He would hope for an audience with the Earl on this occasion. Now that he could no longer return to the inns in Lancashire that he had been frequenting for some time, his need of a loan was becoming more urgent. He didn't intend to stay in Hertfordshire any longer. No doubt the servants there all knew how his wife had treated him. He would be a laughing stock. Arthur bristled at the memory of how Margory had suddenly turned on him totally unexpectedly. It still required thought as to how he would punish her. He had enjoyed doing that by harming his son. Where was Henry anyway? He had been gone for some considerable time now. Perhaps he was dead. Perhaps his captors had killed him when they didn't receive the hostage money they had demanded. How ridiculous to think that he would pay for the return of a child when they were so easy to create. So, on that occasion he hadn't succeeded in forcing Margory. She would regret that. Did she really think he would not make absolutely sure that she obeyed his will the next time he took her? Perhaps he would return to The Manor after all, following his visit to Chatsworth. Someone must know where Henry was. He needed him so that he could force his wife to do exactly as he wished. He would gather all the servants together and, on pain of getting rid of all of them without a reference, he would make sure somebody told him. Yes, his son's absence had gone on long enough. What about Lucy? Did she know, he wondered? Probably not. She was the sort of woman he liked. One who didn't get involved in difficulties happening under her nose. Yes, Lucy was his ideal partner, really. He couldn't go to Marion to find out as, not only would she not tell him – that's if she knew – but her husband would not allow him to insist that his wife told him what, if anything, she knew.

He knew what he would do. He would force that old hag of a servant, Goodwife Sykes to tell him. She knew everything that went on at The Manor, even if she didn't gossip. Pity that. She was one of the few servants he had come across who didn't join in speculation. She was what was called loyal. Well, she would wish she had been disloyal by the time he had finished with her.

Arthur banged on the roof, pleased with his decisions. After his visit to Chatsworth, he would return to Greenwillows, take the old woman, Sykes, aside and show her why it was very unwise to be the good friend of his wife's he knew her to be. That reminded him. In his flight from the inn at Bolton, had he remembered to pick up his pistol? Arthur fumbled around in the pockets of his jerkin. Ah yes, there it was. He breathed a sigh of relief. He never knew when he may have to use it, as he had once before, when defending Margory's parents. And himself, of course. As before, he wouldn't hesitate to use it. On anyone.

Chapter 129

Although the countess never rushed, she was observed by Margory and Hugh to be walking quite quickly towards them, her face knitted in annoyance mixed with frustration.

"I have just received a message from my dear husband that Queen Mary isn't feeling well again, so he is bringing her here with her whole court today, once more."

Margory was immediately concerned.

"Oh, I'm so sorry that we're here, Bess. We can leave right away, if we're an imposition?"

"Certainly not, Margory. This isn't the first time this has happened, although I usually have a little more warning. My staff know what to do and your own are with them. Your friends, Marion and Abner are in their bedchamber and I have sent one of the servants to let them know what is happening. I suggest that you remain in the gardens until Her Majesty and her court have been received into Chatsworth. As you know, the gardens are vast, fortunately, as it takes some time for Queen Mary and her entourage to be accommodated." The countess sighed, prompting Margory to put a soothing hand on her arm.

"Don't worry. Your gardens are so beautiful that Hugh and I are enjoying walking among them, taking in the pretty colours and wonderful fragrances. Forget that we are here, Bess. The Earl clearly knows how very organised you are and understands that you are able to accommodate Her Majesty at a moment's notice. Oh, Bess. Here comes Her Majesty's coach now. I can just see it in the distance."

"Yes, I must leave both of you and shall look forward to seeing you later in the day."

Chapter 130

"Oh Hugh, I have never seen so many guards. But then, Queen Mary is a very precious person who needs to be kept safe. Look at all the different kinds of weapons. You will know what they are, but I certainly don't. I've heard that the longbowmen need to be quite tall as the bows are more than six feet long."

Hugh glanced at Margory, knowing that Arthur was tall, a feature he thought she liked. He had never felt fear which was, he thought, the root of jealousy. No. His love of Margory was not weakened by jealousy.

He looked again at the guards encircling Queen Mary's coach.

"Man behind with weapon!"

The shout was so loud and the guards' response so quick that Margory barely had time to realise at whom this declaration was aimed. It was Arthur.

Quick as the drawing of his pistol was, Arthur's fall was even quicker. Not only did the arrows rain on him, but the pikes and ballock knives were used so fast that Margory had to turn away.

Hugh's arms immediately enfolded Margory, like petals closing at the end of the day.

"Don't look, my darling. Arthur didn't suffer and you won't be suffering any more. You are now free to be with your son. I hope, too, that this marks the beginning of a new life for you and me."

The look that Margory gave Hugh said it all.

PAMELA MANN

Pamela was born in Hertfordshire, England and has also lived in Canada and the USA. Her first exciting experience of being published, at the age of 15, was an article in the local paper on the Greek Parthenon. Since then, she has been an editor of corporate magazines as well as writing articles on many diverse subjects including travel and teeth! She has also taught English, Creative Writing, Memoir Writing and English for people with learning difficulties.

Gradually, her writing has evolved into books, ***Men Rule*** being her third and second historical fiction; ***The Birth of Gossip*** was her first and the up-dated history of an excellent charity was the second. Both historical fiction books are set in the 16th century and her main source of research has been The British Library in London, England.

Pamela is a member of the Society of Authors, the Historical Novel Society and the Arts Society.

Available worldwide from Amazon

Michael Terence
Publishing

www.mtp.agency

mtp.agency

@mtp_agency

Printed in Great Britain
by Amazon

23664528R00162